Minnesota Mediterranean and East European
Monographs

XX

PARTITION THROUGH FOREIGN AGGRESSION

MINNESOTA MEDITERRANEAN AND EAST EUROPEAN MONOGRAPHS
Theofanis G. Stavrou, general editor

Minnesota Mediterranean and East European
Monographs

PARTITION THROUGH FOREIGN AGGRESSION

The Case of Turkey in Cyprus

William Mallinson

MODERN GREEK STUDIES

UNIVERSITY OF MINNESOTA

MINNEAPOLIS, MINNESOTA

Number 20   2010

Minnesota Mediterranean and East European Monographs (MMEEM)

Theofanis G. Stavrou, general editor
Soterios G. Stavrou, associate editor
Elizabeth A. Harry, assistant editor

The objective of the MMEEM is the dissemination of scholarly information about the Mediterranean and East European region. The field is broadly defined to include the social sciences and the humanities. Even though the emphasis of the series is on the Greek and Slavic worlds, there are no thematic, geographical, or chronological limitations. Through the series we hope to encourage research in a variety of contemporary problems in their historical context. In this regard, special efforts will be made to accommodate proceedings from scholarly conferences as well as monographic studies with a diachronic approach.

Monographs in the MMEEM series are published by the Modern Greek Studies Program at the University of Minnesota as supplements to the *Modern Greek Studies Yearbook*. *Partition through Foreign Aggression: The Case of Turkey in Cyprus* by William Mallinson is number 20 in the series. Its publication has been made possible by subvention from the Modern Greek Studies Program at the University of Minnesota.

The price for this volume is $30.00, paperback. Make checks payable to:

Modern Greek Studies
325 Social Science Building
UNIVERSITY OF MINNESOTA
267—19th Avenue South
Minneapolis, MN 55455
Telephone: (612) 624-4526

Library of Congress Control Number: 2010920113
ISSN: 1057-3941
ISBN–13: 978-0-9791218-6-9
ISBN–10: 0-9791218-6-8

Cover: Painting of a Greek olive tree (.1950) by David Mallinson

The UNIVERSITY OF MINNESOTA is an equal-opportunity employer.
Printed in the United States of America on acid-free paper

To the people of Cyprus,
the land of Zeno the Stoic

CONTENTS

LIST OF ABBREVIATIONS

CFSP:	Common Foreign and Security Policy
ECHR:	European Court of Human Rights
ECJ:	European Court of Justice
EEC:	European Economic Community
EOKA:	National Organization of Cypriot Fighters
EMAK:	National Front for the Liberation of Cyprus
ERRF:	European Rapid Reaction Force
ESDP:	European Security and Defence Policy
EU:	European Union
FO:	Foreign Office
FCO:	Foreign and Commonwealth Office
MOD:	Ministry of Defence
NATO:	North Atlantic Treaty Organization
SBA:	Sovereign Base Area
SC:	Security Council
TMT:	Turkish Defense Force
"TRNC":	"Turkish Republic of Northern Cyprus"
UN:	United Nations
UNFICYP:	United Nations Peacekeeping Force in Cyprus

BRIEF CHRONOLOGY

1571–   Cyprus is under Ottoman rule.
1878

1878   The Ottomans lease Cyprus to Britain, following behind-the-scenes machinations by Britain, during which it promises to protect the Ottoman Empire from Russia.

1914   Britain annexes Cyprus as a result of the Ottoman Empire allying itself with Germany in the Great War.

1923   Turkey, under the Treaty of Lausanne, relinquishes all its rights in Cyprus.

1925   Britain introduces a colonial constitution, laden with ethno-religious divisions.

1931   Britain revokes the constitution and introduces direct rule, following rioting and the burning down of Government House, the result of anger at Britain's refusal to recognize the legitimate result of a vote against tax measures.

1955   The National Organization of Cypriot Fighters (EOKA) anti-colonial campaign begins, following Britain's point-blank refusal to discuss the Cyprus question with Greece. Britain hosts tripartite conference to exacerbate relations between Greece and Turkey.

1956   Archbishop Makarios is deported to the Seychelles.

1957   Archbishop Makarios is released from exile, following U.S. pressure on Britain, but is not allowed to return to Cyprus.

1958   Turks instigate anti-Greek rioting in Cyprus.

1959   The Zürich and London Agreements are signed.

1960   Cyprus gains independence, with a set of treaties perpetuating many of the divisive colonial constitutional characteristics.

1963   Britain helps Archbishop Makarios to present his "13 Points" recommending changes to the constitution; Turkey instigates communal troubles.

1964   Turkey bombs Greek Cypriot villages; the Soviet Union warns Turkey not to attack; to Turkey's chagrin, the UN becomes actively involved through the landmark Security Council Resolution 186, which reaffirms the independence, sovereignty, and continuity of the Republic of Cyprus and its government; it also authorizes an international peacekeeping force (UNFICYP) and appoints a mediator for the island, and launches the good offices mission of the UN secretary-general on the Cyprus problem.

1965   Turkey rejects the report by UN mediator Galo Plaza which recommends strongly against division and separation of the two Cypriot communities.

1967   War between Greece and Turkey threatens; Greece withdraws General Grivas and 12,000 soldiers from Cyprus.

1968   UN-sponsored talks are launched between the government of Cyprus and the Turkish Cypriot community.

1972   An Association Agreement is concluded between Cyprus and the European Economic Community (EEC).

1974   Extreme elements of the Greek junta, in conjunction with a tiny anti-Makarios Greek Cypriot minority, organize a coup in Cyprus; the coup fails within days, and constitutional order is restored. Nevertheless, in a massive two-phase military operation, Turkey invades Cyprus and occupies 38 percent of the island.

1977   President Makarios and Turkish Cypriot leader Rauf Denktash conclude a four-point agreement for the settlement of the Cyprus problem under a bicommunal federation, a historic compromise on the part of the Greek Cypriot community in its effort to end Turkey's military occupation and reunify Cyprus.

1983   The Turkish Cypriot leaders declare the illegal "Turkish Republic of Northern Cyprus" ("TRNC"). The secessionist move is universally condemned; the UN Security Council declares it "legally invalid." To this day, it is recognized only by Turkey.

1990   Cyprus applies to join the EEC.

1996   The European Court of Human Rights (ECHR) condemns Turkey for violating the rights of Titina Loizidou in respect of access to her property in the occupied territory.

1998   Accession negotiations are launched between Cyprus and the European Union.

2001   The ECHR condemns Turkey for gross human rights violations in the occupied territory.

2003   Cyprus signs the EU Accession Treaty.

2004   The Annan Plan (V), which would have dissolved the republic and legitimized the Turkish invasion, is thrown out in a referendum; Cyprus becomes a member of the European Union (EU).

2006   President Tassos Papadopoulos and Turkish Cypriot leader Mehmet Ali Talat agree on a new set of principles to guide the Cyprus peace process (the 8 July Agreement). The UN, EU, and the international community at large welcome the agreement.

2008   Cyprus joins the Eurozone; President Demetris Christofias opens direct talks with Mehmet Ali Talat on the Cyprus problem.

2009   Turkish occupation continues; intercommunal direct talks continue; European Court of Justice (ECJ) finds in favor of a Greek Cypriot refugee, ordering a British couple to demolish the property they have built on his land, return the land, and compensate him.

FOREWORD

AS William Mallinson's *Partition through Foreign Aggression: The Case of Turkey in Cyprus* was going to press, United Nations Secretary-General Ban Ki-moon was visiting Cyprus presumably to lend support to his advisor, Alexander Downer, and the participants in the ongoing "intensive talks" for a comprehensive settlement of the nearly half-century-old Cyprus problem. The main participants in these discussions, President Demetris Christofias of the Republic of Cyprus and Turkish Cypriot leader Mehmet Ali Talat, along with their special committees, have been hard at work since September 2008 hammering out details which might insure a viable agreement for the political, institutional, and economic reintegration of the small island state and its people. Yet, anxiety seems to be hovering over negotiators and members of the two communities alike who are fully aware that for historical, geopolitical, and demographic reasons, their political fate has never been an entirely Cypriot matter. This anxiety continues despite repeated pronouncements that current negotiations are rightfully in the hands of the Cypriots themselves. Under-standably, expectations as to the outcome of these talks have ranged widely. Pessimists are resigned to the idea that nothing significant or lasting will result. At best, they anticipate an enforced settlement by outside powers, a settlement that now may even be legitimized by a United Nations endorsement. Opti-mists, on the other hand, are hoping against hope for a solution safeguarding the unitary nature of the Cyprus state, thereby providing institutional and psychological mechanisms for permanent peace.

The publication of Mallinson's book and the negotiations are timely and propitious. In 2010 Cyprus celebrates its fiftieth anniversary of independ-ence from British colonial rule. In the annals of political history, rarely do we encounter demonstrable evidence by which ruling empires willingly and crea-tively contributed to the smooth transition of peoples from dependent entities to healthy successor states. On the contrary, former rulers and occupying powers often serve as formidable stumbling blocks to the whole process. So it was with the young Republic of Cyprus, which joined the family of nations as an independent state in 1960 but was viewed from the start as a "reluctant re-public" or a "fettered" one at best. Though inexperienced at first, the young state's political leadership struggled valiantly to safeguard the island's political independence and expand its economic base. The resilience, indeed the very survival of this small island state, not to mention its success in becoming a European Union member in 2004, is nothing short of miraculous and worthy of serious scholarly study.

For thirty-five of its fifty years as an independent state, the Republic of Cyprus has been a victim of international military aggression by neighboring Turkey. Explanations and justifications for this abound. The sad reality of the situation is that one third of the island's sovereign territory has been under foreign military occupation, the country and its people have been forcibly divided, and one third of the entire population has been displaced from their homes and properties since Turkey's 1974 invasion. As one expert noted,

> The political-demographic de facto partition imposed on Cyprus since 1974 . . . threatens not only the unity and integrity of a modern nation-state but also the millennial cultural integrity and continuity of the island which has been the crossroads of the civilization of the eastern Mediterranean.°

In spite of all this, the international community has been largely silent or inarticulate against a monumental injustice perpetrated by a large and militarily strong neighboring country on a fairly defenseless small state. Worse yet, countries like the United States and Britain, which led the massive world mobilization that reversed Iraq's aggression on Kuwait, in the case of Cyprus took the opposite stand. What's more, they have led the charge to mobilize support for Turkey's accession to the European Union even as Turkey is illegally occupying EU territory. Consequently, they paradoxically reward military aggression instead of putting an end to it. More to the point and relevant to the theme of Mallinson's book, however, is the fact that since the rejection of the deeply flawed Annan Plan (2004) by the Cypriots, persistent pressure has been exerted on the government of Cyprus and the Greek Cypriot community to accept a settlement essentially on Turkey's terms, a settlement invariably and threateningly presented as the last opportunity for a solution to the Cyprus problem, again on a take-it-or-leave-it basis. Experts inform us that under the guise of reunification, such a settlement would leave the country permanently partitioned under an anachronistic apartheid confederal system and would essentially legitimize the results of international aggression. It takes little imagination to appreciate why the government of Turkey is following the current "intensive talks" very closely while promoting its partitionist designs through the Turkish Cypriot interlocutor. Turkey publicly advocates a solution of "two peoples and two states in Cyprus" which may form a partnership under some loose confederal scheme, with strong Turkish guarantees and rights of intervention in the affairs of the Republic of Cyprus. This partitionist design, easily discernible by persons well versed in the complexities of the Cyprus problem, is also reflected in the proposals submitted by the Turkish side as recently as January 2010. Such proposals undermine the agreed basis for the current negotiations under the good offices mission of the UN secretary general for a settlement toward the genuine reunification of Cyprus under a functional federal constitutional structure, as reflected in UN resolutions and in agreements reached by the leaders of the two Cypriot communities since 1977. Turkey's stance against allowing Cyprus to evolve into genuine federa-

---

° Michael Jansen, "Cyprus: The Loss of a Cultural Heritage," *Modern Greek Studies Yearbook* 2 (1986): 323.

tion, favoring instead the perpetuation of the illegal division imposed on the republic since 1974, is an alarming ingredient which may affect adversely the outcome of the current talks.

This latest complication in the deliberations between President Christofias and Turkish Cypriot leader Mehmet Ali Talat lends support to Mallinson's thesis that, throughout the existence of the Republic of Cyprus, the Cypriots have been denied unfettered independence. This is also reflected in peace plans for Cyprus, from the Zurich-London Agreement of 1959 that gave birth to the Republic of Cyprus, to the Acheson Plan of 1964 and the Annan Plan of 2004. The same attitude is reflected in a series of secret moves within NATO, especially in the 1960s and '70s, aimed at either dissolving the republic or preserving it in its peculiar precarious and vulnerable status. In all these moves, the United States and Britain invariably took the side of Turkey. Just as the realities or illusions of the Cold War worked to the advantage of Turkey during the early phase of negotiations for a solution to the Cyprus problem, recent developments in the Muslim world affecting U.S. interests could very well determine priorities and policies toward Cyprus during the current phase of negotiations for a solution to the protracted problem.[†]

Mallinson's book is a warning to the short-sighted policy of great powers promoting the equivalent of partition. It is also a warning to the United Nations and the European Union. Promoting or sanctioning partition, he maintains, will inevitably undermine international legality and decency and will constitute a dangerous precedent of legitimizing international armed aggression. Reasonably, then, he is arguing for a shift away from the partitionist mentality in resolving the Cyprus and other similar international issues. Writing as a historian but with a rich diplomatic background in the British Foreign Service, Mallinson offers in this thoroughly documented work an unabashedly clear course, which can help Cyprus achieve a lasting settlement that will genuinely reunite its territory, people, society, economy, and institutions under a functional federation based on UN and EU principles. Such an arrangement, made possible through a painful and historic compromise by the Greek

---

[†] Despite a flurry of articles in Europe and the United States regarding deterioration of U.S.-Turkish relations in recent years, most commentators hold on to the old formula that this relationship is a vital element in U.S. policy and express the hope that the new U.S. administration will repair recent fissures. A useful study of the evolving nature of this relationship is Stephen Larrabee, *Troubled Partnership: U.S.-Turkish Relations in the Era of Global Political Change* (Rand Corporation, 2010). For a refreshingly insightful account of American policy during the Cold War, see the most recent assessment by Jack F. Matlock, Jr., *Super-Power Illusions: How Myths and False Ideologies Led America Astray—and How To Return to Reality* (Yale University Press, 2010). Among other fascinating observations, the author reminds us that the only time during the Cold War that the Soviet Union and the United States "came close to a nuclear exchange" was "when the United States placed nuclear missiles in Turkey that could reach the Soviet Union, [and] Nikita Khrushchev countered by deploying Soviet nuclear weapons in Cuba. . . . It ended when Khrushchev agreed publicly to remove Soviet missiles from Cuba and Kennedy pledged privately to withdraw the American missiles from Turkey" (20).

Cypriot community in its effort to end Turkey's aggression and reunify Cyprus, can potentially allow all the people of Cyprus to live under permanent conditions of peace and stability, and enjoy the benefits of EU membership with maximum respect for their human rights.

Partition through Foreign Aggression: The Case of Turkey in Cyprus is the tenth volume on Cyprus published in the Minnesota Mediterranean and East European Monographs. In each case, our objective has been to provide a scholarly assessment of an ongoing crisis in its historical perspective. We are delighted to include this study in our series, feeling confident that the author's assessments and recommendations could easily be applied to resolution of other conflicts. It remains for me to express my deepest appreciation to Soterios G. Stavrou and Elizabeth Harry for their tireless efforts and meticulous care as they moved the project through the well-known process of a manuscript in search of a more public life.

Theofanis G. Stavrou
University of Minnesota
3 February 2010

PREFACE

THIS BOOK sets out unashamedly to argue that Cyprus, a member of the European Union, should be a cohesive social and political federation, despite attempts to slice it into two, against the grain of its natural social and historical development.[‡] As such, this book will set out to demonstrate that the very idea of partition for an island state like Cyprus is an unacceptable aberration of common sense and decency, an illicit escape route from commonly accepted norms of international relations, and a bizarre anomaly in the EU context. The current division of the island through the brute force of NATO's second largest army itself highlights the illegitimacy of partition in Cyprus, and how unnatural and contrived the division is, reflecting the anachronistic military goals of a country that is occupying a member of the European Union that it itself is trying to join. To this end, the book will devote the first chapter to a consideration of the term "partition" as applied to the island state of Cyprus, and to how "partition" is simply a cynical euphemism for occupation, forced ethnic cleansing, and subsequent manipulation. It will show how no amount of quasi-academic debate, think-tankery, semantic sliding, and humbuggery can detract from the fact that Cyprus should be reunited through EU and UN law, rather than used as a whipping-boy of the self-seeking strategic obsessions of the worst side of nineteenth-century power politics. The strength, indeed triumph, of the EU legal system has been well demonstrated once again recently through a judgment of the European Court of Justice (ECJ), ordering a British couple to return the stolen land of a Greek Cypriot and pay compensation.

Chapter 2 will trace the vital historical developments so necessary to understanding why Cyprus's present situation is an absurdity, contrasting as it does with European political and social norms. It will help the reader to identify the many mistakes made by large powers in trying to meddle in the affairs of the island. The historical context will be brought up to date, and in turn show the major mistakes made by larger powers in 1960, in granting a form of pretended independence that looks ever more anachronistic as the EU develops and which clashes politically, socially, and morally with international law and undermines the essential principles of the EU.

[‡] I thank Marios Evriviades for some incisive advice on the theme, and for his ability to track down information. In a similar vein, I am grateful to Miltos Miltiadou for his suggestions and criticism of my text, and for his thoroughness and perspicacity.

Chapter 3 will demonstrate how the 2004 Annan Plan was simply a misguided and flawed attempt to perpetuate the division of the island under the guise of a false federation, and to weaken the EU and undermine its future, creating more problems, rather than solving them.

Chapter 4 will juxtapose and compare partition in different parts of the world, showing how often it has been proven to have created, rather than solved, problems, and how Cyprus hardly bears comparison, historically and socially, with many other cases. This is particularly true since, until the deleterious meddling and power politics of various partition-mongers, the people of Cyprus lived side by side in mostly ethnically mixed towns and villages, distributed naturally throughout the island.

Chapter 5 will look specifically at the European, legal, moral, economic, political, and practical arguments against the partition of Cyprus. Some space will be devoted to refuting the flawed and expedient argumentation of partition-mongers, who tend to represent the interests of *partis pris* such as the Turkish military and Henry Kissinger, whose sole objective has been to keep Cyprus as a piece of real estate in an outdated "Great Game."

Chapter 6 will consider the fate of the Turkish Cypriot community of Cyprus, a community whose voice has become increasingly stifled by the illegal importation of mainly Anatolian settlers, who have inundated the original population and are destroying not only the Greek heritage of occupied Cyprus but also the indigenous characteristics of the Turkish Cypriots.

Chapter 7 will draw the strands together, emphasizing the strategic European aspects and exposing the dangers of tactical misinterpretation of the term "federation." In so doing, it will show by default that only a balanced solution in line with EU law and norms will create a functional federation in the interests of Cypriots and the EU, interests which are increasingly mutually inclusive. Chapter 8 will briefly summarize and conclude.

In this book, it goes without saying that the terms "Turkish Cypriot" and "Greek Cypriot" refer only to the native population of the Republic of Cyprus. The terms "Turkish Cypriots" and "Turkish Cypriot community" refer specifically to the indigenous, native citizens of the Republic of Cyprus who are of Turkish ethnic background, and not to the more than 160,000 illegal settlers brought by Turkey into the occupied part of the island after 1974.

Pentagon and the World Trade Center, attacks which merely served to provide emotional fuel to, and intensify, a policy of unilateralism that had already been decided, just as the war on terrorism was being thought out.

If academic and quasi-academic debate helps to present hard-nosed and sometimes extreme policies as reasonable-sounding, that is one thing. The real question, however, is whether the debate leads to wishful thinking, and then action, or vice-versa. In other words, which is the chicken, and which the egg? Whatever one thinks, there is clearly a direct correlation between think-tankery and policy, even if there is a gap between real diplomats and those who study IR. We shall see this when we look specifically at Cyprus.

The large number of theories serves to further muddy the waters. Partition is coming to be a subject of study in its own right, just as its academic master, conflict resolution. Yet the mass of theoretical articles on Cyprus has done little to create a clear picture. If anything, they have avoided some of the most basic issues. One reason is the keenness among political scientists, usually of the behaviorist school, to establish a so-called "conceptual framework" in order to express themselves on paper. They thereby inadvertently imprison themselves in a self-built mental cage of paradigms, models, frameworks, and approaches which can detract from free, clear, and incisive analysis. The result is often the development of a particular theory, or a new sub-theory, leading to the wheel being reinvented for the umpteenth time. Whether we are talking about realism or one of its various branches, about structuralism, normative theory, constructivism, functionalism, modernization theory, positivism, post-modernism, pluralism, dependency theory, world systems theory, or a combination of two or more of these, not to mention the various connected ideas, clarity on the Cyprus situation is not always easy to achieve without a thorough study of the documentary evidence from the past, particularly since the latter tends to confirm many suspicions which were denied at the time by partition-mongers. The following words by Lin Yutang express some of the frustration with too much theorizing:[6]

> Man's love for words is his first step towards ignorance, and his love for definitions the second. The more he analyses, the more he has need to define, and the more he defines, the more he aims at impossible logical perfection, for the effect of aiming at logical perfection is only a sign of ignorance.[7]

This quote does tend to illustrate the tendency on the part of some to disguise their disinclination toward deeper understanding; in other words, covering up intellectual inadequacy and sloth in the interests of image.

On that note, we shall now take leave of the world of IR theory, fascinating and thought-provoking though it can be, and get down to brass tacks, by looking at the nature of the dismemberment of a sovereign state, Cyprus. Let us first look at some of the characteristics.

Cat's Paw

As a victim of externally enforced division, Cyprus is unique, since it is the only island state in the world divided into four parts. One is legal, two (the British territories) legally shaky, while the fourth part is occupied by Turkey and unrecognized by any government except that of Turkey. The Republic of Cyprus nevertheless covers the entire island, with the exception of the anomalous British Sovereign Territories (see below). The divisions are essentially unnatural, given that they do not represent the wishes of the vast majority of the native population; are false economically; run counter to Britain's treaty obligations and the very treaties that were contrived to establish the Republic of Cyprus; and have bedeviled internal communications systems. The military barrier slicing through the republic is unnatural as well as illegal. It is hardly surprising that "The Turkish north depends on agriculture, tourism and aid from Turkey."[8] In this sense, the northern part of Cyprus is a microcosm of its occupier, since Turkey, just like its predecessor the Ottoman Empire in its later years, also depends on massive foreign aid, mainly through the International Monetary Fund, to keep afloat economically, and, therefore, politically and socially.

To say that Cyprus has been, and is, an object of the interests and ambitions of a small number of competing powers is hardly a revelation. In recent times, the major factor has been Anglo-Russian, Anglo-Soviet, and now again Anglo-Russian rivalry, with Britain acting increasingly as the United States' proxy since the Suez crisis of the mid-fifties. The main reason for the unhealthy and intrusive interest in Cyprus is the island's proximity to the Middle East and Asia. Just as it became the Venetian Empire's main military and naval outpost against the Ottoman Empire, so Britain obtained it as a *place d'armes* to watch over an unstable Anatolia,[9] and to combat perceived Russian encroachment in the eastern Mediterranean. An extract from a letter by British prime minister Benjamin Disraeli to Queen Victoria in 1878 gives us the flavor:

> If Cyprus can be conceded to your majesty by the Porte, and England at the same time enters into defensive alliance with Turkey, guaranteeing Asiatic Turkey from Russian invasion, the power of England in the Mediterranean will be absolutely increased in that region and Your Majesty's Indian Empire immensely strengthened. Cyprus is the key of Western Asia.[10]

In a similar vein, and displaying a remarkable similarity in mentality almost one hundred years later, American secretary of state Henry Kissinger was credited in 1976 with the following views: "Dr. Kissinger has frequently spoken of the value of this 'real estate' and the necessity to keep it as a 'British square on the chequer board,'"[11] and "He was also concerned with United States policy over Cyprus on the resolution of the Arab/Israel problem, and he regarded this as more important than Greek hostility towards the United States."[12] Kissinger's mentality can be traced back at least to 1957 and the publication of a book, in which he wrote: "But for the foreseeable future we should be able to count on . . . Cyprus or Libya as staging areas for the Middle East, and on Great Britain as a staging area for Europe."[13] This latter mentality is also to be found in a British paper of 1975:

> We should aim to divorce Cyprus as much as possible from other issues affecting our relations with Greece and Turkey. . . . Turkey must be regarded as more important to Western strategic interests than Greece and that if risks must be run, they should be risks of further straining Greek rather than Turkish relations with the West.[14]

Ever since the Suez debacle, British foreign policy, particularly as regards military policy, has become a subset of U.S. foreign policy. As we shall see, the invasion of Cyprus was a Suez-like watershed in terms of British freedom of action, or, rather, lack of it. British indignation about the nature of Turkish behavior soon gave way to "coordination" with the United States; and when Britain then tried to give up the bases, Kissinger simply said "no!" It is not surprising that de Gaulle said that Britain had no foreign policy of its own. Britain's subservient position to the United States is particularly germane today, as regards Cyprus's future, as it becomes clear that only the EU and, perhaps, Russia have sufficient independence to question Anglo-American hegemony to resolve the question of the illegal occupation, unless Turkey becomes less important than it is for the United States. Today, Britain cannot fire cruise missiles without U.S. permission, while its electronic spying depends on the United States.[15] Most of the Ministry of Defence's research capacity has been bought by a U.S. conglomerate; Britain recently handed over its nuclear research establishment at Aldermaston to the United States, while Parliament was on its Christmas break.[16] It is, therefore, perceived U.S. interests that will be a determining factor in the resolution of the Cyprus situation.

The evidence available, then, shows that Cyprus has been regarded as more of a possession than an independent entity. This "possessive and controlled independence" is an integral part of the Anglo-American policy of keeping the majority and minority groups of Cyprus at loggerheads and to exaggerate their distinctions. It has proven to be the simplest and most expedient way of ensuring Britain's continued possession of its military bases, on U.S. instructions. It also explains why Greek-Turkish agreement over Cyprus is not necessarily useful from the Anglo-American standpoint. Even before the Turkish invasion, the FCO was worried about "Greek-Turkish collusion in an attempt to partition the island," since this could threaten the long-term viability of our bases."[17] Keeping the populations of Cyprus divided to a manageable extent was a useful way of ensuring that Greece and Turkey would squabble with each other, rather than bang their heads together to find agreement. Hence the partition ploy.

But a completely independent Cyprus was also anathema to the outside strategists, to the point of their even considering (in 1964) the usefulness of *enosis* as a way of ensuring the long-term viability of the bases, as the following quote makes abundantly clear:

> From the defence point of view, *enosis*, notwithstanding its obvious difficulties, has certain advantages over the unitary state . . . the risk of Cyprus falling under Russian or UAR influence would be largely eliminated and the retention of our Sovereign Base Areas and other defence facilities might be easier with Cyprus as a province of a NATO ally than with a Cyprus tempted to cash in on the benefits of neutralism.[18]

This apparent readiness to consider *enosis* does, however, need to be qualified. The idea was that it would be a useful way of preserving the British bases, and, on top of that, giving Turkey a chunk of Cyprus, with a base. This was hardly genuine *enosis*, but rather a subtle form of multi-partition.

The main point to emerge from this brief look at Cyprus's status as a "key," "*place d'armes*," "staging area," "piece of real estate," and "square on a chequer board," in the words of the armchair strategists, is that the power-brokers interfering in Cyprus's destiny had, and have, as we shall see, only scant interest in democracy, human rights, and self-determination outside their own countries, even though they use the terms sufficiently often as to render them double-speak. In so doing, they disguise, first, the fact that their solutions are more imposed than democratic, and second, that their perceived interests constitute the backstage reality, with the people of Cyprus as whipping boys. Hence, as we shall see, the panacea of promoting intercommunal talks, but only as long as the interests of the power-brokers are protected, which understandably include preventing war between Greece and Turkey. A cynical, but nevertheless perceptive, quote by a British diplomat serving in Cyprus in 1976 throws matters into relief:

> In my view, the merit of the inter-communal talks is that there is no danger of their leading to a Cyprus constitutional settlement. There never has been any such danger, ever since the talks began in 1968 . . . one should not, in deference to the island's mythical sovereignty, independence and territorial integrity, insist on re-complicating matters with constitutional structures.[19]

It should by now be reasonably clear that, despite Cyprus's EU membership, the territory of the island is still far more important to the Anglo-Americans than the actual inhabitants, who appear more of an irritant than an asset. This is a reflection of the geopolitical mentality of which Cyprus, and indeed its whole region, is an object. This crude pseudo-science (described by one expert as a primitive form of international relations theory produced largely by geographers),[20] once used to justify Nazi policy and brought back into vogue by, among others, Kissinger, tends to divide the world into areas (called "regions") based on resources but ignores natural frontiers. Hence the obsession with oil and gas and the concomitant importance of the Middle East to strong powers; and hence Cyprus's invidious position in this whole geopolitical merry-go-round.

Our analysis will, therefore, proceed from the starting point that despite Cyprus's perceived independence (or perhaps because of the possessive nature of its independence), the island as a whole has not been able to choose its own independent path to a sufficient degree, despite being a nominally sovereign state, for the simple reason that it is the victim of armed aggression and a continuing occupation that flies in the face of European norms and values. Its membership in the European Union has, however, put an entirely fresh complexion on matters which is beginning to cast serious doubts on the whole approach to the problem by Cyprus's so-called guarantor powers. Let us now turn briefly to the question of "ethnicity," a politically emotive term these days, which is often used by the promoters of partition to justify their views. We include here, of course, religion, language, and culture, so often part of the whole baggage accompanying the debate on partition.

Demographic Exploitation

It is hardly a secret that during times of international instability, the ethnic card is played strongly by indigenous populations and outside powers alike. In the case of Cyprus, the evidence points very much, as we shall see, to outside interference and manipulation as the prime culprits of the tensions which occasionally broke out on the island, following Britain's takeover. The Ottoman Empire had the habit of settling various Turkic peoples in conquered territories, with the Balkans being the main recipient. Cyprus was no exception, with the settling of Turkish-speaking settlers in the sixteenth century, most of them janissaries.[21] One can draw a parallel here with the export of Scottish Protestants to Roman Catholic Ireland, at a time of great tension between the two churches, the unfortunate results of which were to manifest themselves in no uncertain manner, then as today. Yet in the case of Cyprus, far from the religious wars (ethnic wars were not the order of the day, at least overtly) that ravaged whole swaths of Europe, the populations existed side by side during the Ottoman tenure, with the majority Christian Orthodox population running many of its own affairs. This was a far cry from the repressive policies of the English masters of Ireland who had to cope with periodic rebellions and all manner of opposition, the flavor of which remains to this day. As we shall see in the case of Cyprus, the creation of "sides in a dispute" was essentially a British invention, which still today casts its anachronistic shadow over the island. Certainly, the Ottomans managed to plant the seeds of future strife throughout the Balkans, through population transfers and religious conversions (the Bosniaks bear witness to this), whether forced or not, not to mention periodic bouts of savagery.[22] Cyprus, however, was spared most of the chaos and cruelty that resulted from the demographic manipulation of the Balkan region by Venetians, Austro-Hungarians, Russians, Ottomans, and later French and British. Because Cyprus remained in the firm grip of the Ottomans, and then of the British administration, it does not bear easy comparison with the Balkans, where old entities (and enemies) were hurriedly cobbled together in 1918, amid a combination of local romantic nationalism and power-broking among the French, British, and Italians, with the Americans trying to promote their Wilsonian idea of democracy in Europe (which sat rather strangely with their treatment of blacks and Red Indians in their own country).

As we shall see, most imposed partitions, rather than solve problems, have led to future problems. Kashmir is a case in point, as is Palestine. The Middle East, as a whole, provides a particularly poignant example of the dangers of big powers carving out zones of influence, witness the secret Sykes-Picot agreement of 1916. The Iraq-Kuwait problem, for example, can be directly traced to this arrangement, just as the outbreak of fighting in Palestine and its subsequent partition in 1948 can be traced to incorrect and expedient interpretation of the Balfour declaration and Britain's "taking French leave" (and pulling out early, into the bargain).[23] Few would dispute the contention that many of the international relations problems with which the world is confronted today have their origin in large powers having divided up areas of interest, often manipulating populations, with little regard for local sensitivities and realities. Had the British not encouraged the emigration to Uganda of thousands of Indians, they and their descendants would not have suffered persecution and expulsion at the hands of Idi Amin in the early seventies. Matters are compounded when large powers actually seek to create and then exacerbate division in order to maintain control. And this is the case of Cyprus, as we shall see. Before Britain began to seek ways of hanging on to the island, Greeks and Ottomans had lived side by side and intermingled for hundreds of years.

Conclusions

We have seen how, despite the alleged progress of the human race and periodic grand declarations by grand people, such as "New World Order" and the like, the same negative human characteristics tend to return with different colors. The tendency to divide is one example of this. The words of an expert sum up the nature of partition:

> Whether undertaken as an expedient or as a panacea, the outcome of recent political/geographical partitions has been generally uniform; they have either proven inadequate and sometimes dangerous as expedients, or, instead of providing panaceas, have frequently compounded the very problems they were intended to resolve. . . . While the partition experience has been generally an unhappy one for the peoples involved, it seems to have been due, in the colonial context, to the *native* prejudices and hatreds which were cultivated *before* partition and, in the Cold War context, to the suspicions and rivalries of *outside* parties *after* partition.[24]

In the case of Cyprus, and the obsession by certain outside powers to exploit it as a strategic chess piece, we see that the island has been the object of both colonial and Cold War considerations. Partition can, in the case of Cyprus, be seen to be a euphemism for invasion and occupation. One is tempted to wonder whether the word "partition" should be applied to Cyprus at all, since it diverts attention away from the fact that it is nothing more than an illegal invasion and massive ethnic cleansing operation. Another expert sums matters up nicely:

> Partitions are perverse: they achieve the exact opposite of what they nominally intend; they increase conflict. First they cause conflict that accompanies the partition, and such conflict is consistently worse than that which preceded it. In raw numbers, the critics [of partition] are correct across the cases of India, Palestine, Ireland and Cyprus.... Partitions are especially perverse when they have domino effects—triggering post-partition wars and insecurity.[25]

Lest anyone even begin to attempt to apply the platitudinous label of "conspiracy theory" to this book, it is important to state now that this author is particularly skeptical about both "conspiracy theory" and the tendency to use it as a label for those who reveal embarrassing truths. Every conclusion in this book is based on painstaking documentary research and the consequent revealing of documents, many of which are used here for the first time, having only been recently released, sometimes following considerable pressure and recourse to the British Freedom of Information Act.

CHAPTER TWO

The Ottomans and the British

*I should not produce any British plan or proposal until a Greek-Turkish deadlock
has been defined.*[1]
Permanent Undersecretary of the Foreign Office, June 1955

Introduction

Cynical though it may sound, Cyprus offers a fascinating case study of
how people can be manipulated by outside interests. In this chapter, we shall
first juxtapose Ottoman and British rule, and then see how the British manipulated the people of Cyprus to ensure that they maintained their strategic
interests in the island, even after the controlled independence that Cyprus
achieved after 1960. We shall scrutinize those 1960 arrangements, and the
causes and reasons for the breakdown that occurred, mentioning Foreign
Office doubts about the treaties and the bases. We shall consider the run-up to
the invasion and the methods used by Kissinger to ensure that it occurred.
Space will be given to President Makarios's initiative of 1977, and how san-
guinea the British high commissioner was about it. The conclusions will
home in on the massive, illegal, atavistically Ottoman demographic
manipulation by Turkey, to try and create a *de facto* situation, thus rendering
serious talks a near-Sisyphean task.

The chapter will concentrate mainly on those aspects relevant to the
idea of dividing populations. It will arm readers with the necessary and relevant history to enjoy the main body of the book, namely, comparisons with
other partitioned areas of the world, and how the Turkish occupation has
negatively affected Cyprus, international relations, the *raison d'être* of the
European Union, and Middle Eastern stability. Readers may wonder why I
have included the period after the qualified independence that Cyprus gained
in 1960, when the chapter is entitled "the Ottomans and British." This is because, owing to the large number of strings attached to the settlement in the
form of the treaties and Britain's military rights, Britain—and the other "guarantor powers"—retained rights which detracted from complete sovereignty. As
such, Cyprus is still, to a certain but crucial extent, British, and, therefore,
American, given the latter's control of British Middle Eastern policy. We shall
discuss this at greater length in chapter seven.

The Ottomans

When the Ottomans conquered Venetian Cyprus in 1571, one of their first acts was to import thousands of janissaries and Anatolians to Cyprus as settlers. This was replicated throughout many territories conquered by the Ottomans, as we can see today, for example, in Thrace and Bulgaria. The Ottomans were generally more interested in raising taxes than in interfering in the religious lives of those whom they had subjugated, ruling through the *millet* system, whereby the Christian Orthodox Church ran its own affairs, particularly in education. The Christians of Cyprus were, of course, second-class citizens, although their status began to improve in the dying decades of the Ottoman Empire, thanks to Russian influence and the *Tanzimat*, a series of liberalization measures introduced throughout the empire. At about the same time as the Ottomans were exporting settlers to Cyprus, British (mainly Scottish) Protestants were landing in Roman Catholic Ireland, thereby sowing the seeds of future strife there. During Ottoman rule in Cyprus, there was rarely, if ever, strife between the ordinary Christian and Muslim populations, and certainly nothing on the scale of Oliver Cromwell's massacre of Roman Catholic priests, women, and children at Wexford and Drogheda, events still remembered today. Cypriot Christians and Muslims lived side by side, scattered throughout the whole island. The office of *dragoman* (interpreter) assumed increasing importance in the later years of the empire. The invariably Greek holder of the office acted as a powerful mediator between the Christians and the Ottoman authorities. Apart from occasional bouts of slaughter, as in 1821, the Ottoman period was one of sleepy social stability. There was no partition of Cyprus under the Ottomans. Although they planted alien seeds in conquered territories, a fact which was to be exploited negatively by outside powers in later years, physical partition *per se* was not part of the Ottoman system. Things were to change with the arrival of the British, who were confronted with one of the Ottomans' most significant bequests, namely, a strong Church of Cyprus, which would lead the quest for independence and union with Greece.

Union

Independence *per se* had not been a serious desire of the Cypriots, since with the independence of the Greek state, the essential wish of the native (and vastly superior numerically) population of Greek stock was to unite with the homeland, as many Greek populations had managed to do, and would continue to do until 1947, both in territories adjacent to freed Greece and in islands. Cyprus's problem in this respect was its geographical location far from Greece, but near to Anatolia. The Turkish-speaking Muslim population, in stark contrast, had no distant homeland with which they could identify to any great degree, since Turkey did not exist until 1923, even if the term "Turk" had been used increasingly, as the Ottomans and other Turkic tribes made Anatolia their home. The early Cypriot struggle for independence was essentially a wish to unite with Greece, although this would later change to a desire to simply be independent, and master of oneself. There was no wish on the part of the Muslim Cypriots to unite with Anatolia, which was itself a myriad of different peoples, only becoming a state in 1923.

Britain's aim in procuring Cyprus was essentially strategic, to "watch over an unstable Anatolia,"[2] protect it from Russian expansion, and thus increase British power in the Mediterranean. Possessing Cyprus also helped Britain to protect Suez. Such considerations were not, however, relevant to the wishes of most Cypriots, who simply wished to forge their own destiny. They were strengthened in this by their new-found equality with the Muslims which was, of course, thanks to the more democratic administrative methods of the British.

Disproportionate Division

Dividing the population of Cyprus was not yet an overt part of the British agenda. Although at first their treatment of the locals was even-handed, showing no particular favoritism, the method of administration, particularly when Cyprus passed to full British control and became a crown colony in 1925, was that while the Cypriots were treated equally, they were divided unequally. Thus, in the Legislative Council, the British officials and Muslim representatives balanced the Christian Orthodox representatives. Since the high commissioner had the casting vote, this meant that, in effect, 18 percent of the population could frustrate the wishes of the majority. The Legislative Council was, then, essentially a sop to democracy. More importantly, it represented a form of hidden constitutional apartheid, with its religious, racist, and linguistic divisiveness. Thus, the novelty of the British form of colonial "democracy" began to wear off quite quickly for the vast majority of Cypriots of Greek tradition. Conversely, the Muslim population came to see the British as their guarantee against being incorporated into the Greek state, a fact which would be exploited by the British to an increasing extent. It was with the arrival of the British that the concepts of Greek and Turk were systematically applied in Cyprus, even though Turkey did not exist as a state.[3] In its internal correspondence, the British authorities constantly referred to "Greek," "Turk," "Greece," and "Turkey," thus laying, inadvertently or otherwise, the psychological foundations for future strife and division.

By the turn of the century, pressure for *enosis* was strong, with some leading Cypriots of Greek stock even suggesting that British rule was worse than Turkish:

> The Turkish despotism, in spite of its coarseness and arbitrariness, was free of the deceitful hypocrisy and, when it had satisfied its financial wants and the base covetousness of its corrupt Government, it allowed the subject races to enjoy the blessings of their soil and intelligence and never thought of laying snares for their nationality. . . . Turkish despotism . . . paid respect to the religion, the language and the nationality and kept subjugated nations stationary, but intact and

never thought of exterminating or injuring them by the use of force or through hypocrisy, as the pharisaical and hypocritical tyranny of the English does nowadays.[4]

The British correctly identified the church as the main promoter of independence and *enosis* and, therefore, proceeded to try and dilute its power, particularly through interfering in education:

> By exercising a hypocritical tyranny the English Occupation in Cyprus has put down the privileges of the Church and of our holy clergy . . . the English Government add now an undisguised treacherous attack on our national education, not only through hidden operations and advices, but also through an absurd and unjust persistence in entrusting the inspection thereof to an English priest who is entirely unacquainted with the Greek language and is ignorant of the pedagogue science.[5]

Following the union of Crete (with a sizeable Greek-speaking Muslim minority) with Greece after the Balkan Wars of 1912–13, *enosist* rioting took place in Cyprus, resulting in five deaths and one hundred thirty-four injured.[6] The Great War then intervened to dampen the fervor, which nevertheless continued after Cyprus became an official Crown Colony in 1925, culminating in major rioting throughout the island and the burning down of Government House in 1931. This was followed by the revocation of the colonial constitution, which was never to return, although it would be replaced on independence in 1960 with what many would term a neo-colonial constitution. The spark for the rioting, it should be noted, was the refusal by Britain to recognize the rejection by the Legislative Council of a taxation measure. This underlined the undemocratic nature of British rule: even a constitution designed to accentuate the distinction between the majority and minority groups, and to ensure that the minority and the ruling power could veto the majority, could not ensure that the British always got their own way. The most poignant part of the whole affair was that it was thanks to a (minority) Muslim member of the council that the vote went against the colonial power. He became known as the "thirteenth Greek." The revocation of the colonial constitution nipped in the bud any serious and unfettered future Greek-Turkish Cypriot institutional cooperation, which was, and still is, anathema to the British and then the Americans, since it could have led to a genuinely independent and possibly neutral Cyprus, thus wrenching the island from the hungry hands of the geopolitical strategists.

Underground

The harsh measures taken by the British, combined with the then Greek prime minister, Eleftherios Venizelos's, controversial policy of playing down the question of Cyprus to maintain good relations with Britain and Turkey (the latter expressed in the friendship treaties), meant that *enosis* went underground. In Greece, however, support for *enosis* began to grow, particularly after Venizelos went into exile in 1935. Although overt opposition was difficult in Cyprus, the question began to attract strong support in Athens, with the establishment of the "Society of Friends of Cyprus." When the celebrated British historian Arnold Toynbee weighed in favor of *enosis*, the Foreign Office managed—for a while—to suppress publication of an article of his.[7] In another article, Toynbee wrote:

> The protection of the local Turkish minority has ceased to be a formidable problem now that Greece and Turkey have buried the hatchet. . . . The choice lies between staying in Cyprus and losing face or leaving Cyprus and adding to the honours which we won for the British Empire when we left Wei-hai-wei in 1930 and the Ionian Islands in 1864. We do not regret that Corfu and Ithaca are under the Greek instead of the British flag today. This Ionian precedent for British policy towards Cyprus is singularly apposite.[8]

Despite these sentiments, the rigid Colonial Office did not seriously consider leaving Cyprus. However, the British sweetened their attitude during World War II, since they needed soldiers. They even went as far as to use the slogan "For Greece and Freedom," which fed, whichever way one looks at it, *enosist* hopes. Thirty-seven thousand Cypriots flocked to the recruiting stations, of whom one third were Muslims.[9] This is a very high number for such a small population, some 12 percent of the total. The sentiments expressed, and policy advocated, by Toynbee were reflected in considerable measure among senior British government officials after World War II (which, like its predecessor the Great War, again intervened to dampen overt action for *enosis*).

Division through Fear of Communism

It is perhaps a paradox that Cyprus, that most Greek of islands, did not undergo the horrors of the Greek Civil War that raged on the mainland until 1949. A paradox, because it was largely due to British control of the island, however undemocratic, that the warped and artificially contrived right- and left-wing extremism nurtured in Greece hardly affected Cyprus. Britain fought with the nationalist and anti-communist forces, until handing Greece to the Americans in 1947. At any event, Britain's role, particularly Churchill's obsessive support for the return of the king in the face of the wishes of the majority of Greeks, exacerbated the divisions in Greece. The divisions, fanned by the very actions of British troops against its former Resistance allies, were an ominous example for Cyprus, where Britain would encourage divisions between Greek-speaking Christians and Turkish-speaking Muslims, rather than between communists and anti-communists. As we shall now see, the civil war also provided the British with a convenient excuse not to give up Cyprus.

As early as 1945, Francis Noel-Baker, a prominent member of parliament, had written to the British secretary of state, advocating the union of Cyprus with Greece to strengthen Greece in the struggle against communist forces.[10] A senior official agreed.[11] Two years later, a senior Foreign Office official advocated *enosis*.[12]   The response was that there was a danger of a communist regime in Greece by Christmas 1948, if the Americans withdrew.[13] This was nonsense, since it was the British who had withdrawn, handing Greece over to the Americans. Inconsistency of argument seems to have been the order of the day: on the one hand, give up Cyprus to strengthen the fight against communism, but on the other, keep Cyprus to do the same! Despite the U.S.- and Soviet-promoted decolonization that was taking place, the UN's emphasis on self-determination, the giving up of India, the impending British pull-out from Palestine, and the handing of the Dodecanese to Greece, Cyprus bucked the trend, owing, apparently, to specious argumentation about communism.   This was despite considerable American irritation with Britain's increasingly rigid position. At any rate, the horrors of the Greek Civil War, in which Britain was so involved at the beginning, perversely served to make it easier to justify hanging on to Cyprus.

The Seeds of Division

Although British policy had not thus far been one of consciously dividing the population of Cyprus, or of manufacturing antagonism, a new and cynical course now began to be adopted, even before the 1950 church-organized plebiscite, in which 96 percent of Greek Cypriots voted for *enosis*. At the end of 1947, a Foreign Office official wrote: "Finally, though the Turkish government has never raised with us any questions affecting the Turkish minority in Cyprus, this minority should be protected."[14] Significantly, the official who wrote the paper incorporating the statement worked for the secret Information Research Department, Britain's equivalent of the Soviet Cominform, responsible, *inter alia*, for propaganda. Thus, even before matters came to a head, the British had decided to use the Muslim population of Cyprus as a Turkish minority, despite the fact that the Turkish government had never even raised the question. From then on, Britain refused to budge from its rigid position, while the Greek government became increasingly frustrated. The newly elected Archbishop Makarios of Cyprus, armed with the results of the plebiscite, began a round of overseas journeys taking in the United States, Britain, and Greece. In September 1953, the British foreign secretary, Anthony Eden, refused to even discuss the question of *enosis* with the Greek government, leading to considerable anger, with the Greek government claiming entire liberty of action in promoting *enosis*. Gone were the Venizelist days of avoiding the problem. In July 1954, a British Cabinet paper concluded:

> We must, therefore, act on the assumption that deterioration in our relations with Greece is the price we must pay if we are to keep Cyprus. A point may even come at which we should have to decide whether Cyprus is strategically more important to us than Greece.[15]

Two months later, in what could be easily construed as a barely concealed threat as well as an example of imperial *rigor mortis*, the British minister of state, Selwyn Lloyd, told the UN General Committee:

> The Turkish-speaking Cypriots, who are Moslems, are bitterly opposed to Enosis . . . As I say, there has up to now been no communal strife. Does the assembly [General Assembly] really want to stir it up by keeping this matter on the agenda?[16]

Division through Secret Collusion and Black Propaganda

The diplomatic gloves were now off. Britain, knowing full well the moral and legal weakness of its case and worried about U.S. criticism of its inflexible stance, began to woo Turkey by helping it with its arguments. The following extract from a letter by the British ambassador to Turkey in February 1955 shows us the tip of the hidden and murky iceberg:

> Turkish representatives abroad, particularly in London and Washington, might be more active in their publicity about the Turkish attitude to Cyprus. In the United Kingdom, their efforts might be directed (in this order) to a) Members of Parliament, b) the weekly press (they have already been helped by the journalists' visit last year). The same appears to be true in the United States and other countries. Turkish propaganda should however be presented with tact. For example, the Turkish Press Attaché in London has done no good by distributing leaflets of the "Cyprus is Turkish Association."
>
> This has already been discussed in general terms with officials at the Ministry of Foreign Affairs . . . Secondly, the Department might be able to encourage a few selected Members of Parliament to come here on their own initiative, to learn something of Turkey generally and the Turkish attitude to Cyprus in particular. . . . The Turks will no doubt be glad to know in due course what policy H.M.G. propose to follow between now and the next meeting of the United Nations General Assembly and Turkish policy is likely to be influenced by British views.[17]

The Foreign Office did its utmost to conceal its bias in favor of Turkey:

> Our attitude to this [Cyprus] question is that we wish to assist the Turks as much as possible with the publicity for their case, but must at the same time be careful not to appear to be shielding behind them and to be instigating the statements.[18]

An important part of Britain's secret campaign involved black propaganda, in other words, outright lying and gross exaggeration, normally only used in war: "I have considered that this task would be better performed by the selection of an officer from outside Cyprus possessing expert knowledge of propaganda methods, including clandestine or 'Black propaganda.'"[19]

The British were at the same time as their secret collusion with the Turkish government maniacally lobbying the Americans, in order to keep the question out of the UN. It was during this period of secret British collusion with Turkey that the only recourse open to the Cypriots and their Greek mainland supporters came to be seen as direct military action: on 1 April 1955, Colonel George Grivas's National Organization of Cypriot Fighters (EOKA) began its guerrilla campaign against the British colonial authorities.

The British reaction was to prepare for what can only be described as a diplomatic confidence trick, as we shall see: a trick that had, and still has, enormous repercussions on Cyprus and its region. It paved the way for the future dissection of the island, if not by express design at the time, then at least by default.

Divide and Keep

Knowing the weakness of its case, Britain's immediate aim was to keep the Cyprus issue out of mainstream UN discussion, so as to continue to hang onto Cyprus. The Foreign Office therefore decided not only to help Turkey (as it was already doing) but to give it an official role in Cyprus's future. This was in direct defiance of the Treaty of Lausanne, by which the new state of Turkey had given up any rights in territories formally under the jurisdiction of the Ottoman Empire. In a *tour d'adresse* of semantic chicanery, Britain decided to invite the Greek and Turkish governments to a conference on "Political and Defence Questions, as concerning the Eastern Mediterranean, including Cyprus." Although the title of the conference was designed to suggest that Cyprus was not the prime focus, this was a travesty of the truth: in fact, the conference was simply designed to ensure that Britain would hang onto the island, as the foreign secretary told the Cabinet: "Throughout the negotiations our aim should be to bring the Greeks up against the Turkish refusal to accept *enosis* and so condition them to accept a solution, which would leave sovereignty in our hands."[20]

One of the chief protagonists in the whole tawdry affair seems to have been the permanent undersecretary of the Foreign Office, Ivone Kirkpatrick, who minuted to his minister of state on 26 June 1955:

> I have always been attracted by the idea of a 3 Power Conference, simply because I believe that it would seriously embarrass the Greek Government. And if such a conference were held, I should not produce any British plan or proposal until a Greek-Turkish deadlock has been defined . . . The plan I like least is that alleged to be reiterated by Mr. Selwyn Lloyd [Minister of State] viz. an enquiry of the Greek and Turkish Govts. Whether—if the island reverts to them—they would guarantee us the necessary military facilities. This seems to imply that we are reconciled to handing over the island to one of them—and that it is up to them to decide on the future of the island. And I repeat: I shall not produce any British plan until a Greek-Turkish difference has been exposed.[21]

Needless to say, the Turkish government accepted the invitation with alacrity, while the Greek government dithered for another two days after the Turkish acceptance. According to the evidence available, the Americans convinced the Greek ambassador to the United States that Turkey was only being invited as a witness.[22] Whether the Greeks accepted through extreme naïveté or lack of judgment is still a moot point, but once they had, the secret British-Turkish collusion intensified. Prime Minister Eden wrote patronizingly of the Turks (whom both the Colonial and Foreign Offices seem to have considered docile and, therefore, malleable): "Turks are behaving well. If we keep friendly with them, the Greeks will have to come along in the end. Therefore, we must not be parted from Turks, though we need not be ostentatious about this."[23] The Americans, for their part, knew what was going on: "Since British undoubtedly know what position Turkey will take at Conference, their tactics are obviously designed to force Greece to define its attitude."[24]

Much has been written about the Turkish-inspired riots (which the British appear to have known would happen),[25] the wanton destruction of Greek property and livelihoods in Turkey, and the end of the reasonably correct Greek-Turkish relations that had existed since 1930. Suffice to say that they occurred as the conference blew up.

The Americans Step In

It was by now quite clear that the British, under their increasingly unstable and emotional prime minister, Eden, were unable to cope with the situation on their own, unless they were to give up Cyprus, lock, stock, and barrel, which they were not prepared to do. Although they had Turkey on their side, that was not enough. The Americans now began to prepare plans that would involve independence, while retaining British military rights in Cyprus. The Suez crisis, in which the United States (and the Soviet Union) pressured Britain and France to cease their attack on Gamal Abdel Nasser's Egypt, marked the transfer of control of the Middle East from Britain to the United States. Since Britain's Middle Eastern Headquarters, in particular its electronic eavesdropping operations, had been transferred to Cyprus, the American objectives were to ensure that Britain maintained its military presence in Cyprus and prevent war between Greece and Turkey, which the impulsive and ill-thought-out British policy had so nearly caused. At this stage, the Americans were more benign and detached than the British. Concerned at the state of emergency and the exile of Archbishop Makarios to the Seychelles, and at the full-scale emergency, in which a few hundred EOKA guerrillas were holding down forty thousand British troops,[26] they drew up a proposal whereby the British would agree to a truce and the Cypriots would run their own internal affairs for ten years, and would then hold a referendum to decide on union with Greece, local autonomy under the Greek Crown, full independence, or self-governing status under British sovereignty, all with guarantees for the minority. The paper pointed out that the "Turkish minority" in Greece had been well treated by the Greek authorities.[27] However, British intransigence, their insistence that EOKA surrender, and their refusal to deal with the exiled archbishop killed the plan in its embryonic form. The British nevertheless realized the precariousness of their position, but more particularly, of the Turkish case. The British Statistical Service wrote: "report shows the decline of the Turkish population [of Cyprus] from about one quarter to about one fifth—which does not really help the Turkish case very much."[28] Hence Britain's free tuition to the Turks, and, more overtly, such measures as hiring hundreds of extra policemen who were, of course, Turkish Cypriots; allowing the establishment of a "Cyprus is Turkish Association," when Greek political parties were banned; and, generally, showing considerable bias towards their "well-behaved Turks."[29] A recalcitrant Britain (for so it must have seemed to the perplexed Americans), now under pressure, put forward the so-called Radcliffe proposals, which were rejected by Greece. They would have entailed local autonomy, with the possibility of independence later, but only, as the secretary of state for the colonies told Parliament, if the Turkish Cypriot community were given the freedom to decide its future status.[30] In this sense, it is likely that this form of self-determination would have opened the door to partition, particularly given the way in which Britain had been colluding with, and coaching, Turks and Turkish Cypriots alike.

U.S. pressure increased: the British were constrained to release Archbishop Makarios (in April 1957) but did not allow him into Cyprus, a move which brought him yet more international respect than he had already gained through being exiled (shades of Nelson Mandela). Still they continued to beat about the self-determination bush, in the full knowledge that Turkish policy was by now partition, at the very minimum. The Turkish Cypriots were now fomenting considerable trouble through their armed fighters, the Turkish Defense Force (TMT): on 7 June 1958, a Turkish or Turkish Cypriot *agent provocateur* planted a bomb in the doorway of the Turkish Consulate's information office.[31] When it exploded, Turkish Cypriots went on an anti-Greek rampage, and many Greeks had to leave their homes. Over one hundred were killed,[32] including eight Greek Cypriots out of a group of thirty-five dumped by the British near a Turkish Cypriot village. This left a sour taste, which was not forgotten in later, post-"independence" troubles. The last governor of Cyprus, Hugh Foot, wrote of the Turkish foreign minister:

> [Fating] Zorlu, the Foreign Minister of Turkey, was the most ruthless of them and was, I think, the rudest man I ever met . . . He had, I have no doubt, known of and perhaps given the orders for the Turkish riots and the attempt to burn Nicosia.[33]

The anti-Greek rioting was all grist to the mill of Turkey's attempts to partition Cyprus and bode ill for the future. The Macmillan Plan was the next effort to achieve a settlement, but it would have involved a tridominium of Britain, Greece, and Turkey. Its last version was rejected by Greece and accepted by Turkey. It was just before Britain attempted to impose the plan that Archbishop Makarios broke the vicious circle, by letting it be known that he would forego *enosis* and accept independence, under UN auspices, to avoid the possibility of partition. This irritated Turkey, which had been hoping for partition, hence their support for the Macmillan Plan. The archbishop realized that although genuine independence was not on the agenda, it would at least be a start, and was infinitely preferable to the dissection of his country. His intervention, although embarrassing to Britain and unwelcome to Turkey, nevertheless put the cat among the pigeons, and at least put a stop to overtly partitionist plans. But it was the beginning of a war of diplomatic attrition, and worse, which continues to this day.

We shall not deal at any length with the niceties of what led to the 1960 qualified independence that Cyprus achieved, since this has been adequately covered in numerous books and articles. Suffice to say that the patriotic yet realistic archbishop later wrote that the least "bad thing was to sign."

The Poisoned Darts of Division of 1960

The world over, different groups of people live together separately, having learnt how to live and let live. In Britain, go to Wolverhampton, and you will find that most of its areas are inhabited by those of Pakistani and Indian stock, Muslim and Hindu into the bargain. In the Brixton area of London and the St. Pauls area of Bristol, the majority of the population is of African stock. In Greece's Western Thrace, Muslims, mostly of Turkish stock, rival Christians in numbers and must be envied by the Turkish Cypriots. On the Greek islands of Rhodes and Kos, there are several thousand Muslims of Turkish stock, all speaking Greek and Turkish. Apart from some racial rioting in Bristol, in the Notting Hill Gate area of London, and in the Toxteth area of Liverpool some years ago, there has never been the remotest possibility of civil war or of being forced to leave your home. The groups live happily side by side, respecting each other's differences. They may not as a rule mix socially or intermarry, except when and if they feel inclined to do so as individuals. In the United States, the election of an African-American president speaks volumes for equality of opportunity, whatever the occasional bouts of tension, themselves usually the result of bigotry and racism, dying phenomena. Studying at school and university alongside Christians, Muslims, Hindus, and Jews and working alongside different people can be enriching intellectually, as long as one is not forced together unnaturally, in which case, just as on a crowded train, tensions can increase.

In post-Medieval Cyprus where, it should be noted, the Muslims were spread over the whole island, there were never serious problems between peoples, other than the occasional tensions provoked by developments overseas. Then the British arrived. But it was not until they began to clumsily tinker with the very spiritual essence of the Christian Cypriots, the church, through the latter's responsibility for education that the average Christian Cypriot began to get testy. Even then, there were no serious intercommunal problems until the British made it quite plain that they meant to promote the nationalist aspects of the Muslim community and began to implement their divisive tactics and woo Turkey, thereby provoking the anger of Athens.

Before we now briefly consider the divisive aspects of the 1960 arrangements, it is important to bear in mind that, whether by default or design, the above-mentioned anti-Greek riots of 1958 quite understandably created the conviction among the Greek Cypriots that they were very much on the defensive vis-à-vis an Anglo-Turkish alliance, and that the riots had left them with a justified feeling of having been the oppressed underdogs, despite the fact that they constituted the overwhelming majority. Most important, sections of both the Greek and Turkish Cypriots had been manipulated and radicalized. Thus, although there was temporary euphoria at being "independent," the reality of partition would soon rear its ugly head. Before we show how divisive the 1960 arrangement was, a number of points need to be made.

First was the obvious fact that the Cypriots were hardly involved in determining their own future: Archbishop Makarios, only allowed in to the negotiations late in the day, was presented with a *fait accompli*. He spent much of his energy in whittling down the size of the territories demanded by Britain. The fact that the Cypriots were hardly involved in deciding their own future contrasts vividly with the protracted talks that London had with, for example, the Irish, Indians, and, later, the Seychellois. It is clear that Cyprus was simply seen as a *"place d'armes,"* and that its people were merely considered as tools in the works of meta-colonial military strategy.

Second was the fact that the main, albeit hidden, purpose of the treaties that created the republic was Britain's permanent retention of two parts of Cyprus. Hence the absurdity of fifty-six of the one hundred and three pages of the Treaty of Establishment being devoted to Britain's territories and a whole plethora of connected rights which detracted from the idea of sovereignty in the real sense of the term. An ominous parallel can be drawn here between Cyprus and the Chagos Islands, which Britain bought from pre-independence Mauritius, then throwing out the inhabitants to make way for a U.S. base on Diego Garcia, which Britain had rented to America (see chapter 5, 66-67).

Third was the fact that, despite the Greek prime and foreign ministers' responsibility in accepting a deal involving official Turkish participation, their government as a whole was unhappy with Britain's efforts to involve Turkey. Before the fateful Zürich agreements, the British ambassador to Greece wrote: "The Greeks are angry at the UK plan to involve the Turks . . . on the grounds that it introduced an element of Turkish governmental intervention . . . and since it must lead to further antagonism and eventually to partition."[34] They were to be proven right. What, however, apart from the illegitimate involvement of Turkey, whose policy was already, at the minimum, a federation leading to partition, were the poisoned darts of division?

First, the constitution was based on an extreme form of positive discrimination, based essentially on perceived ethnicity amounting to constitutional apartheid, and therefore promoting division from the word go: despite the fact that the ratio of Greek to Turkish Cypriots was 82:18, the ratio was 70:30 for the civil service and 60:40 for the police and the armed forces. The House of Representatives was also organized on an apartheid basis of 70:30. Crucially, on any question of importance such as one affecting the municipalities, separate Greek Cypriot and Turkish Cypriot majorities were required, meaning that the minority could thwart the majority: hardly a principle of democracy. In short, the internal constitutional structure of Cyprus was insulting to democratic principles and prevented the smooth running of the state, amounting to a complete denial of the rights of the majority. As a future president said in 1969, the provision for recruitment of employees in the public service offended not only every notion of equality and democracy, but also numerous international conventions concerning employment without discrimination on account of race, religion, or sex.[35] Any form of positive discrimination is in fact insulting to its intended beneficiaries, since it assumes that they are handicapped in some way, and not equal to the rest.

Second was the fact that the crucial grassroots question of the organization of the municipalities in the big towns was to be left to post-independence negotiations. It was this, above all, that led to the breakdown, a breakdown strongly hinted at by the British high commissioner.[36]

Third was the Treaty of Guarantee, which included, at Turkish insistence, the fateful sentence: "In so far as common or concerted action may not prove possible, each of the three guaranteeing powers reserves the right to take action with the sole aim of establishing the state of affairs created by the present treaty." In 1974, Turkey would interpret this clause over-expediently: it had been awaiting, in any case, its opportunity to pounce and create partition through force. It is interesting that not only did the Cypriot government point out that the treaty was contrary to the United Nations Charter, but the Foreign Office itself, as we shall see in chapter 5, when we discuss, *inter alia*, legal aspects. The Foreign Office legal advisers were, indeed, contradictory about the whole treaty package.

Fourth, and perhaps contradictorily, the Treaty of Guarantee forbade both *enosis* and partition. The very fact that it did so highlighted the danger of the stipulation being ignored in the future, as indeed proved to be the case. Moreover, the inclusion of such self-evident stipulations underlined the shakiness of the whole quasi-legal pack of cards. As for Britain, it appears that it had never intended, as we shall see, to honor the Treaty of Guarantee, preferring to hide behind the Americans, who had no legal role in Cyprus. Although the 1960 arrangements cannot *per se* be directly blamed for the subsequent collapse, their very nature, and the manner of their application, certainly afforded Turkey and the radicalized Turkish nationalist elements of the population the opportunity to pursue their partitionist aims. The mystery is how any serious-minded person could believe that such an arrangement would not lead to almost immediate problems. Many of the treaties' provisions were a monkey on the back of the freedom and independence of the island, just as much of the constitution was an anachronistic extension of Britain's colonial pre-1931 ethno-religious administration.

Towards Apartheid

The troubles and self-imposed apartheid initiated by the Turkish Cypriots in 1963 have been capably covered in numerous books and do not need to be described in detail here. A number of points do, however, need to be made.

First, when Archbishop Makarios tried to amend the constitution to make it more workable and democratic, the Foreign Office actually helped.[37] Its behavior was curious, since even the most naïve analyst could have predicted the extreme Turkish reaction by not involving the Turkish Cypriots early on in the negotiations. Second, despite the proposals' reasonableness (for example, abolishing the right of veto of the president and vice-president of the republic, modification of the proportion of Greek and Turkish Cypriots in public service to correspond to the ratio in the population of Greek to Turkish Cypriots, and unification of the administration of justice), Ankara rejected them even before the Turkish Cypriots had had a chance to consider them, and to negotiate.

Third, the fighting that followed was Turkish-instigated. Turkey, for its part, had long harbored partitionist aims for Cyprus and, as we have seen, even wanted the island back, were the British to vacate Cyprus completely. In 1955, Turkish foreign minister Fatin Zorlu said that Cyprus must belong to a "country like Turkey."[38] The following year, the Turkish government's special advisor on Cyprus wrote that if the British did not leave Cyprus, it should be partitioned.[39] In 1963, three months before the Turkish rejection of President Makarios's British-sponsored constitutional amendments, the resultant anti-Greek rioting, and auto-ghettoization of the Turkish Cypriots, a Turkish Cypriot report, signed by the vice-president, Fazil Küçük, and the president of the Turkish Cypriot Communal Chamber, Rauf Denktash, referred, *inter alia*, to forcibly concentrating the Turkish[40] community in one area, and to increasing to the maximum the Turkish population of the island, through the arrival of people from Turkey as tourists.[41] At any rate, when the rioting started, the Greek Cypriots fought back with gusto, memories of the pre-independence anti-Greek riots still raw. Because the Greek Cypriot irregular forces had overrun the Turkish Cypriot ones, the Turkish government was later able to initiate a propaganda campaign claiming that the Greek Cypriots had a plan to annihilate the Turkish Cypriot population. This plan, known as the "Akritas Plan," was, however, simply a typical contingency plan, mysteriously "found" and exploited by the Turkish Cypriots to bedevil intercommunal relations. Some years later, in 1977, after the Turkish invasion, a similar document was "found" and castigated by the Turkish Cypriots but exposed by FCO officials as based on a propagandistic lie. Typically and, it must be said, somewhat hypo-critically, the FCO officials kept their comments to themselves. An extract from a letter by a diplomat at the British High Commission in Nicosia is sufficiently damning as to obviate the need for analysis:

> [A]nod indeed the passages of the documents actually reproduced, are highly selective. The key question . . . is the exact translation of the phrase represented by the Turks as "extermination". The word literally means "cleaning out", and in the context refers I think simply to the flushing out of pockets of resistance, whether military or guerilla, but with no specific reference to the civilian population. . . . The Defence Adviser has been carefully through the whole document

and has discussed it at length with the US Embassy. His conclusion and theirs is that the documents are at least genuine, that the Greek units named correspond with the order of battle which obtained at the date in question, and that the whole plan is no more than contingency planning in the event of an outbreak of fighting initiated by the Turks. The Turkish Government and the Turkish Cypriots will undoubtedly make the most of their propaganda effort . . . possibly in the Strasbourg context, but it may not make all that much impact.[42]

Fourth, just as the British officer responsible for liaison between the Greek and Turkish Cypriots, Lieutenant Commander Martin Packard (see below), was about to achieve success in organizing the return of the (mainly Turkish) Cypriots to their villages, the whole project was abruptly terminated, and he was flown out of the island on an American aircraft. This was because the Americans had simply told the British that partition was the best option.[43] Moreover, as we have seen, the British and Americans would not countenance Greek-Turkish agreement over Cyprus, since this could threaten the existence of the bases. We shall discuss Britain's attempts to give up the bases in chapter 5. Fifth, and connected to the above, is the fact that Britain had lost its freedom of action in foreign and military policy vis-à-vis the United States.

Sixth, the British and Americans had agreed that they would not prevent a Turkish invasion (whatever their official admonitions), as the following makes abundantly clear:

> The Americans have made it quite clear that there would be no question of using the 6th Fleet to prevent any possible Turkish invasion . . . We have all along made it clear to the United Nations that we could not agree to UNFICYP's being used for the purpose of repelling external intervention, and the standing orders to our troops outside UNFICYP are to withdraw to the sovereign base areas immediately any such intervention takes place.[44]

Seventh, it was Soviet threats towards Turkey that gave the partitionists cold feet. As a result of the threat to help Cyprus, President Johnson issued a stern warning to both sides not to take matters further.[45] This did not, however, prevent the *de facto* partition that had now begun and which would be taken to an extreme in 1974. Eighth, it was the involvement of the UN, thanks mainly to Soviet pressure and President Makarios's skill and international prestige that, to Turkish anger, led to a temporary *status quo* and the frustration of Ankara's attempts to partition and annex the island, or part of it.

The Rejection of Galo Plaza's Common Sense and Ten Tense Years

The involvement of the UN at least created a veneer of peace, but only a veneer because, under the surface, Turkey was angry at the official ignoring of the Turkish Cypriots as a separate entity (somewhat hypocritical, since Cyprus was recognized as a whole, not as Greek or Turkish Cypriot); because Grivas (see chapter 2) had returned to Cyprus; and because the British kept a low profile while the Americans promoted double-*enosis* and partition, in the shape of the so-called Ball-Acheson plan. It must be stressed here that Grivas was far more palatable to the Americans than to President Makarios,[46] because of his strong anti-communist credentials and the idea that he might well contemplate some form of double-*enosis*. Makarios was understandably very skeptical, since he wished for an independent Cyprus. The United States' real aims were exposed when Assistant Secretary of State George Ball told Martin Packard, the above-mentioned officer responsible for mediation between the Greek and Turkish Cypriots: "Very impressive, but you've got it all wrong, son. Hasn't anyone told you that our objective here is partition, not reintegration?"[47] To rub the salt into the wound, on the eve of the implementation of the reintegration plan in which he had played a central role, Packard was whisked out of Cyprus on an American C-47 transport, as the sole passenger, while the plan was dustbinned.[48] One expert sums up the saga succinctly:

> The Acheson Plan of 1964—indicative of the typical arrogance of great v. small power diplomacy—would remain the basis for negotiations between Greece and Turkey over Cyprus for the next ten years. Acheson's proposals had implied contempt for a disobedient small state and its leaders; it represented a classic example of *realpolitik*,[49] where, in many ways, people are a secondary concern.[50]

Ominously, "Acheson-Ball-type thinking" was to continue, contributing to the shenanigans surrounding the 1974 extremist Athens-engineered coup in 1974 and the concomitant Turkish invasion. Similar thinking also surrounded the dangerously destabilizing Annan Plan (see next chapter), but Cyprus was spared any further Turkish aggression, thanks in part to the EU and Turkey's application to join it.

During the 1963–64 troubles, the Foreign Office, for its part, seriously considered both the unitary state and even *enosis*, as a way of ensuring that its bases would remain unscathed:

> [A]lthough *enosis* is in some respects more attractive than the unitary state, Turkey's objections to it are so strong that it may not be a practicable solution at present . . . efforts should be concentrated on easing the path to the unitary state, e.g. by providing UN safeguards for the minority and by giving financial and other assistance to the resettling of those Turkish Cypriots to whom Cyprus may no longer appear a tolerable home.[51]

This common sense did not, however, prevail, suffering the same fate as UN mediator Galo Plaza's report of 26 March 1965. The report came as a bombshell to the Americans and Turks, since it essentially rejected the idea of the Turkish-proposed federation (often a euphemism for partition), questioned the 1960 treaties, suggested demilitarization, and advocated continued independence. It also rejected double-*enosis*, irritating to promoters of the Ball-Acheson plan. They rejected the report.[52]

It is fair to say that the unwise outright rejection of the Plaza report had a deleterious effect. Although, outwardly, there was an uneasy calm, backstage, the forces were jockeying for position and straining at the leash. The return of Grivas to Cyprus and the build-up of Greek forces, together with the strengthening of the Turkish forces, was a powder keg, made yet more volatile by the military coup in Greece. The junta included a number of *enosists* spoiling for a confrontation, just as was Turkey. Archbishop Makarios, on the other hand, was simply interested in the unfettered independence and integrity of Cyprus, rather than *enosis*. By this time, the idea of *enosis* had in any case mutated in many minds into a euphemism for double-*enosis*, where Turkey would have had a considerable chunk of territory. In other words, *enosis* would have been another form of partition. In November 1967, fighting broke out, sparked by the Turkish Cypriots.[53] The United States exerted enormous pressure on Greece and Turkey to avoid all-out war, and Grivas and the soldiers had to return to Greece. It was the subsequent emphasis on intercommunal negotiations that were to prevent another explosion, at least until 1974. Despite these negotiations, which became something of a *sine qua non* to simply keep the lid on rather than find a real solution, and despite Turkey's rigid position on a separate status for the Turkish Cypriots, by the summer of 1974 the negotiations were proceeding well, with expectations of some kind of breakthrough. Indeed, had the negotiations been able to continue, unencumbered by outside interference, there is a chance that the Cypriots would have come to an agreement. Interestingly, while Britain and the United States publily seemed to endorse these UN-sponsored intercommunal talks, they engaged Greece and NATO in secret parallel talks within NATO without the involvement of the Cypriots, in order to reach their own kind of settlement on Cyprus along partitionist lines.

The 1973 Polytechnic anti-junta riots in Athens had, however, led to an unstable and particularly anti-Makarios military regime in Greece, masterminded by the fanatic Dimitrios Ioannides, resulting in the failed coup in Cyprus that gave Turkey the long-awaited pretext to invade, after Britain had refused to live up to its responsibilities and intervene jointly to restore the state of affairs created by the Treaty of Guarantee. This showed how dangerous that treaty was, what a misnomer the Treaty of Alliance was, and what a para-constitutional mess the whole 1960 affair had turned out to be. Galo Plaza had been right on the mark in his report, but common sense was now dangerous to the proud, selfish, and fanatical forces in play, both abroad and in Cyprus.

Cementing Partition through Invasion and Occupation

Much has been written about the Turkish invasion and occupation of Cyprus, and it is not our purpose to go over old ground, but rather to filter out those aspects that clearly show the efforts on the part of certain protagonists to partition Cyprus, rather than to achieve a democratic solution based on equal rights for all, without ethno-constitutional apartheid. This will enable the reader to connect more efficiently with the arguments against partition which we shall deploy later on. The most bizarre aspect is that, in considering a solution after the 1963 breakdown, Britain was prepared to seriously contemplate, as we have seen, both *enosis* and partition, both expressly forbidden in the treaties that it had signed. This expedient ability to ignore aspects of the treaties, while laudably being a tacit admission that the treaties were otiose, bode badly for the British government's attitude before and during the Turkish invasion. A number of points need to be made.

First, following the coup, Britain refused to take joint action with Turkey, thus giving Turkey a pretext to act alone.[54] To its credit, Britain did try and persuade the Turks to attend a meeting of all three guarantor powers, but the Turkish prime minister, Bulent Eçevit, refused to recognize Greece as a guarantor. Second, Kissinger tried to delay seeing Archbishop Makarios in his capacity as president of Cyprus, but was finally frustrated in this:[55]

> Kissinger seemed puzzled as to why we were working to move so quickly and in such absolute support of Makarios . . . it was surely a mistake to commit ourselves now to Makarios and thus narrow our options when it was far from certain that Makarios could return to power.[56]

Third, Kissinger pressured the British not to insist on the withdrawal of Greek officers in the Cypriot National Guard, thus further exacerbating the situation and egging on the Turks.[57] Fourth, the Foreign Office knew, via the Joint Intelligence Committee, about the Turkish invasion plans before the first landing: "The situation envisaged below is an invasion of Cyprus by Turkish forces in the next few days in accordance with the JIC expectation of the Turkish plan of operations."[58]

Fifth, in the two days before the invasion, the Foreign Office refused to cooperate with the French by giving them information. The French realized that the Americans were not exerting pressure on Greece to pull out their officers.[59] Sixth, Kissinger procrastinated, in order to give the Turks as much time as possible to plan and consolidate their invasion. Here, some quotes make matters undeniably clear. Just after the Turkish landing on 20 July, Kissinger wrote to Callaghan:

> [O]ur Ottoman friends cut loose . . . it is essential that we work closely together in all of this so that we do not set in motion any train of events before we have a precise view of what we want to achieve . . . if pressure from the outside should be brought to bear to restore Makarios, this will only solidify the regime in Athens.[60]

Seventh, during the frenetic tripartite negotiations in Geneva, British prime minister James Callaghan was informed in detail by the Assistant Chief of Defence Staff (Operations) about the Turkish plan to invade and take over one third of the island, and expressed his concern.[61] Nineteen months later, in the presence of two FCO advisors, he lied, saying that he had had no indications of a Turkish invasion.[62] To have told the truth would have irritated the Americans. More to the point, such an embarrassing revelation would have bedeviled his preparations for the premiership.

Eighth, when Callaghan asked Kissinger on the day of the major Turkish attack on 14 August whether he could attend a NATO meting, Kissinger agreed, "as long as it was not held before Monday 19 August."[63]

This was to give the Turks more time: they had achieved their objectives by 18 August. Ninth, on 14 August, on the telephone Callaghan told Kissinger:

> Well, I was just thinking—I think in military terms, obviously the Turks will carry on until they have got this line they have figured out on the map, and cynically, let's hope they get it quickly . . . You're not going to act, we're not going to act unilaterally and the UN is going to get out of the way.[64]

Tenth, on the day of the invasion, a senior State Department official wrote to Kissinger: "Assuming the Turks quickly take Famagusta, privately assure Turks we will get them a solution involving one third of island, within some kind of federal arrangement."[65]

From a position of studied indignation when Turkey invaded, the British government quickly succumbed to Kissinger's dictates, and, as with the questionable Suez debacle, ended up looking rather indecisive and supine. The difference with Cyprus is that, unlike in the case of Suez, Britain had a legal obligation to intervene. One quote, above all, sums up the reality of Britain's position then, as now:

> We should also recognise that in the final analysis Turkey must be regarded as more important to Western strategic interests than Greece and that, if risks must be run, they should be risks of further straining Greek rather than Turkish relations with the West.[66]

This bias was particularly evident when Britain flew directly to Turkey those Turkish Cypriots who had congregated in the British base at Akrotiri following the Turkish invasion. In doing so, they were also helping to solidify the Turkish partition plan, since the Cypriot government was trying to negotiate an agreement with the Turkish Cypriots.[67]

The British government's supine and confused position vis-à-vis the invasion was well summed up two years later by the Select Parliamentary Committee on Cyprus: "Britain had a legal right to intervene, she had a moral obligation to intervene, she had the military capacity to intervene. She did not intervene for reasons which the government refuses to give."[68] To rub salt into the wound of partition which he had administered, and before he left the U.S. administration, Kissinger threw in a final dart of partition in the form of the so-called "principles initiative," which was resisted for a while by the French. Its key similarity with the Annan Plan was the third of its five principles:

> Simultaneously with agreement on territorial modifications, the parties will agree on constitutional arrangements for the establishment of a federal system on a bizonal basis with relatively autonomous zones which will provide the conditions under which the two communities will be able to live in freedom and to have a large voice in their own affairs, and will agree on the powers and function of a central government.[69]

This was nevertheless a characteristically vague statement, in that "relatively autonomous zones" could be interpreted in several ways.

Kissinger's Central Role

The above evidence shows that, while he may not have actually conspired to divide Cyprus, Kissinger simply schemed and procrastinated to allow the Turkish armed forces the time and diplomatic space to achieve their objectives, knowing full well that the result would be partition. It is hardly surprising that he wrote that the Cyprus problem was solved in 1974. Various pro-partition academics have tried to exonerate Kissinger from any dark role in the 1974 fiasco, first, by being studiously, or intellectually sloppily, unaware of such documentary evidence that we have shown above and, second, by believing Kissinger's memoirs, to the effect that he was not really closely involved in the Cyprus crisis. In an allegedly joint paper, two political scientists claim that Kissinger did not see Cyprus as a priority.[70] They also claim, without real evidence, that the communications facilities and the Sovereign Base Areas did not merit the importance attributed to them by the "conspiracy theorists," apparently unaware of the importance (see above) that Kissinger attached to them, and of the pressure he exerted on a reluctant Britain to keep them. Another academic (who works at the Eastern Mediterranean "University" in occupied Cyprus), apparently keen to exonerate Kissinger, even claimed that there was no communication with the British prime minister on 20 July, the day of the invasion.[71] Yet the secretary to the Cabinet wrote: "Between 1445 and 0700 [on 20 July] the Secretary of State for Foreign and Commonwealth Affairs spoke twice to Dr Kissinger and summoned the Turkish, Greek and Soviet representatives to London."[72] Kissinger also sent a message to Callaghan that day, replying to one from Callaghan. It began: "As I promised you by phone, here is the message you and I discussed. I was about to send it to you when our Ottoman friends cut loose."[73]

It is unfortunate that some academics, keen to promote a partitionist point of view, cannot even do their homework properly. This sort of sloppy research goes hand in hand with sloppy viewpoints. Perhaps the most accurate judgment of Kissinger comes from a senior British diplomat:

> It is impossible to square Kissinger's expressed views with reality... It is rather his manner of conceiving foreign policy without reference to, or knowledge of, the State Department or anyone else which is most worrying. It leaves one with the fear that any day something could go seriously wrong because the normal sources of advice, restraint and execution are wholly by-passed.[74]

Something did go seriously wrong, undoubtedly helped by Kissinger's *modus operandi*. It is significant that he was not a trained career diplomat. Apart from the above damning references to the amateur diplomat, further insight into Kissinger's *modus operandi* can be gained from several publications.[75]

The Continuing Impasse

Given the evidence presented in this chapter, it is obvious why the intercommunal negotiations, officially initiated in 1968, have yet to achieve a permanent solution. The main reason has been Turkish intransigence, often silently supported by Britain and the United States in the name of their version of western interests. The purpose of this book is not to analyze those negotiations: the subject has in any case been dealt with at length.[76] Even when President Makarios agreed in early 1977 to an independent, non-aligned, and bicommunal Cyprus, thus giving away a lot psychologically to the Turkish Cypriots, nothing happened. We shall never know if it would have, since he died that summer. The British high commissioner did, however, write that Makarios represented the best hope of reaching a settlement.[77] Perhaps rather farcically and contradictorily, during the course of the years of negotiations, the Turkish Cypriots continued to consolidate their autonomy and import from Turkey thousands of illegal settlers, who now outnumber the Turkish Cypriots by two to one. In 1983, they illegally declared the "Turkish Republic of Northern Cyprus," recognized (illegally) to this day only by Turkey. At any event, the following Foreign Office quotes, perhaps rather contradictory in view of British support for the United States and Turkey over Cyprus, show the real reason why the negotiations have foundered time and time again:

> It is tiresome that the Turkish Cypriots are behaving in this aggressive and pettifogging way (Their obsession with percentages is perhaps illuminating in connection with the causes of the breakdown in inter-communal negotiations 1960–1963!).[78]

> And the Turkish Cypriots, supported by Ankara, have consolidated their hold on the north to an extent that makes them more than ever reluctant to yield anything near the minimum acceptable to the Greek side as a basis for a settlement.[79]

> The prime minister said that his experience of the Turks was that they pocketed whatever was offered and asked for more.[80]

Thus, we see here how big was the gap between what the British thought and what they actually did. As with Britain's desire to give up the bases (see chapter 5), it was to the United States that Britain turned, rather than be its own master, in the style of the French.

Conclusions

The central point which emerges from this chapter is that in 1974, Cyprus was, for the first time in its history, divided through armed force, with 200,000 of its people forced from their homes to pave the way for the massive ethnic import that followed. Cyprus's Muslim and Christian inhabitants had lived amicably together for nearly four hundred years, before strategic colonialism and power politics reared their ugly heads, with the artificial introdiction of exaggerated radical nationalist tendencies to a malleable population that was then championed by a large but volatile state, Turkey, with the crucial support of Britain, simply to maintain as much of a grip on Cyprus as possible, with not only Turkish, but American help. If we have learned anything so far about the nature of the attempted permanent partition of Cyprus, and perhaps worse, it is that international law does not sit easily with power politics. We also see that while fear of, and rivalry with, the Soviet Union provided the excuse to keep Cyprus, this is still the case, despite the alleged end of the Cold War, which was about interests, with ideology being the excuse.

The resilience of the Cypriots, and their attachment to the law rather than politically expedient solutions (the word "political" often being used as a euphemism for "illegal"), has, however, served the cause of future unity well, thanks to Cyprus's membership in the European Union; but it has also complicated the issue, since Cyprus is now not only an instrument of Anglo-American defense policy (see chapter 7) but also of Turkey's bid, supported by the Anglo-Saxons, to gain membership in the organization. But the new threat of Cyprus being held hostage to Turkey's EU aspirations, as well as to foreigners' strategic ambitions and Turkey's claims on Greek sea and islands, could well be an opportunity, if handled in a strictly legal and EU context. To fully understand the nature of the obsessive attempt to keep Cyprus divided, or at least to make it into a theoretically united but weak *de facto* protectorate, and before reaching the major part of this book, namely, the arguments against partition, we need to consider certain aspects of the Annan Plan, since it was conceived as a way of avoiding a fully-fledged EU solution to the island's problems and of maintaining partition in the guise of federalism.

CHAPTER THREE

The Annan Partition Scheme

Senior members of the Bush administration have suggested an improved deal on the
UN package for northern Cyprus to the Turkish military in return for Turkey's cooperation in providing bases and logistics for any US-led war against Iraq.[1]

Introduction

The historian A. J. P. Taylor wrote that we learn from history how to
repeat our mistakes. Perhaps that is why, in the words of the Renaissance historian and statesman, Guicciardini, the past sheds light on the future, things
have always been the same, and the same things return with different colors.
The so-called Annan Plan is no exception, its very conception based on a studied ignorance of the lessons that should have been drawn, lessons that had
been heeded by Galo Plaza but then swept under the carpet of expediency and
interests that had little to do with the interests of the population of Cyprus.
This chapter will not be an exhaustive analysis of the whole fraught and at
times farcical process that led to the plan's death, but will, rather, home in on
its inherently divisive aspects, to demonstrate how it was simply a desperate
attempt by Britain, the United States, and Turkey to continue to maintain their
perceived interests in Cyprus by weakening any central and independent foreign policy and security role, and by nipping in the bud the potential influence
of the European Union. For a good, detailed analysis and evaluation of the
scheme, readers can turn to Claire Palley's seminal work.[2]

Reasons for the Scheme

What triggered the scheme was Cyprus's impending membership in the
European Union in May 2004.[3] With a member state occupied by an applicant (or even a supplicant), it would have been ridiculous to expect Cyprus, or
indeed any member, to support Turkey's application. The United States and
Britain therefore considered it vital to kill any possibility of Cyprus and, by
extension, Greece, from exercising a future veto on Turkish membership. This
was particularly the case, since the stronger the EU became, the more embarrassing Turkey's position would become, and the more likely Cyprus's future

participation in the Common Foreign and Defense Policy would be (even if it only involved planning). This would in turn have rendered Turkey's claims on some Greek islands yet more surrealistic than they are. The linkage with Turkish interests had already become obvious in 1995, when the EU was forced to accept Greece's insistence that Cyprus be granted official applicant status, in return for Greece agreeing not to veto a customs union with Turkey, which then went ahead. Thus, we see how the whole question of Cyprus's very right to exist is contingent on a range of external issues that are difficult not to take into account, let alone avoid. In order to keep Turkey's application looking serious, Britain and America decided that it was vital to legitimize an (illegal) occupation that was already proving increasingly incompatible with civilized European norms. Since Greece had bravely made it clear that it would veto the whole mass entry of the ten new members if Cyprus were to be denied, Britain and the United States had no choice but to introduce the hidden partition scheme.

Logically, legally, and morally, the solution to such a problem would have been for Britain and America to put pressure on Turkey to simply withdraw from Cyprus, thereby resolving the main problem at a stroke. But this would have strengthened the EU's future clout in the eastern Mediterranean, detracting from Anglo-American control, already threatened by a resurgent Russia. Above all, the existence of the anachronistically named British Sovereign Territories would have been called into question, which would of course have helped Russian interests, and by extension Syria. Indeed, it could have undermined U.S. and British efforts to invade Iraq. This would in turn have worried Israel, which depends on American and British support far more than on that of an often critical European Union. Hence the need to ensure that when Cyprus joined, it would be as an emasculated member, unable to use its membership to introduce European norms into the whole island. For this would have weakened Turkish and, therefore, Anglo-American influence.

The first reason, then, for the Annan scheme, was that Cyprus's membership posed a threat to perceived Anglo-American interests, which of course depended on the bases and Britain's other perceived rights. These rights were not compatible with European Union norms.

The second reason, a subdivision of the first, was to ensure that Turkey, considered important to the United States, was not weakened or angered, since it was necessary to U.S. Middle Eastern strategy. In short, the United States and Britain wished to accommodate the wishes of the Turkish military, which is the final arbiter in Turkey, intervening at will to prevent serious attempts to make the country more democratic, to the extent of toppling elected governments. Thus, the Turkish military pursued a disingenuous and double-faced tactic of supporting the broad aims of a bizonal, bicommunal federation, while telling the Turkish Cypriots what to do, and directly demanding through the Ankara government that the UN make last-minute maximalist demands to support its strategic wishes, demands that it knew would be rejected by the Greek Cypriots—in other words, to support reunification, but only on their terms, while continuing to consolidate partition.[4]

The third reason, also connected to the above, was the planned attack on Iraq, where the United States and Britain were desperately wooing Turkey.

In the words of one expert, it was clear that Turkish concerns, beginning in 2002, over the direction of the U.S.-led Coalition war in Iraq and fears for the impact of the outcome of the war on Turkish security, played the most sig-indicant and continuing role in the Turkish General Staff's insistence that the Annan Plan be deliberately made to fail.[5] The Turkish military was obviously keen to use the Iraq crisis to consolidate its hold on Cyprus, while paying lip-service to unification. This reduced the whole scheme to a blatant attempt at international window-dressing, where style won over substance, thereby reducing the plan to a disguised form of further partition, and probably further strife. The late president Tassos Papadopoulos put matters eloquently but realistically when he wrote that the plan would have established a complicated and dysfunctional state, through continuous deadlocks on clearly political is-sues unsuitable for judicial arbitration, which would have led, with a high de-gree of certainty, to paralysis, with the distance between paralysis and dissolu-tion being very short.[6] This could obviously have been exploited by Turkey, which had, after all, originally invaded Cyprus at a moment of instability. It could have found any number of shallow pretexts to occupy the rest of Cyprus.

The fourth reason, more of a serendipitous concomitant one from the Anglo-American viewpoint, was that, by perpetuating Cyprus's divisions and weakening its decision-making power, the scheme would undermine tradi-tional EU principles and integrationist tendencies, which have always been anathema to Britain, except for the brief period of Edward Heath's premier-ship. This was particularly true in defense, where the British, with the Americans behind them, have been pushing for NATO to be all-powerful, with only a NATO-dependent European Security and Defence Policy (ESDP) allowed to operate "when NATO is not engaged," rather than a fully-fledged integrationist Common Foreign and Security Policy. Connected to this was the fact that Turkish membership in the union would reduce the latter to an unwieldy and floppy trading body, far too disparate in nature to ever merge into a political force strong enough to seriously challenge Anglo-American in-tersest in the Middle East.

The above also explains the flurry by the Anglo-Americans in December 2001 to sign with Turkey the so-called Ankara Agreements, where-by they agreed that Turkey would have a say in any putative ESDP operations in the eastern Aegean and around Cyprus. Although the agreement was signed without EU authorization, the latter eventually agreed to keep Cyprus out of ESDP operations. Greece then secured additions to the agreement, whereby, somewhat farcically, no NATO member would threaten the use of, or use, force against another NATO member. This was hardly a declaration of con-faïence among NATO members! In other words, by reference to the eastern Aegean, some islands of which Turkey illegally claims, the Turkish military was using Cyprus to keep Greece and the rest of the EU from having military responsibilities within the EU borders between Greece and Turkey.

The fifth reason, or perhaps motive is an apter word, was to try and force through the plan to help Turkey's application to the EU, which would have led to the fatal weakening of the organization. On the one hand, Turkey and its sponsors hoped that the Greek Cypriots would be cajoled into accepting a dodgy and dangerous plan that would have benefited Turkish and

U.S. interests to the detriment of the Cypriots. On the other, if (as must have been obvious to even the most inexperienced observer) the plan was rejected, then Turkey would appear to be the PR winners, which would have helped their EU application, as they tried to depict the Greek Cypriots as obstructive. In other words, Turkey saw an opportunity to have its cake and eat it, whatever the outcome, even with the second best option of rejection.

Further Partition

The above is the context in which we can understand that the Annan Plan was no more than a scheme to perpetuate and legitimize the partition of Cyprus, to achieve the strategic aims of the United States, Britain, and Turkey. The ground had already been prepared when, following UN secretary general Kofi Annan's announcement on 11 November 2002, David Hannay, the British diplomat wheeled out of retirement to promote the scheme, somewhat brusquely presented it to President Glafkos Clerides four days later. The following eighteen months were a surrealistic pastiche of transmogrifying plans, ending up with Annan arbitrarily inserting his own finishing touches to the fifth version of the scheme, which largely reflected last-minute Turkish desires, particularly partitionist in nature. The most blatant giveaway of the whole confidence trick was the constant pressure from Britain and the United States on Greece, Turkey, and Cyprus to sign the Foundation Agreement. First, the latter essentially resuscitated the divisive 1960 arrangement, about which the Foreign Office legal advisers had been equivocal and had had considerable doubts (see chapter 5); second, it reaffirmed the existence of the British territories, which Britain had actually tried to give up in the aftermath of the Turkish invasion (see also chapter 5); third, and particularly blatantly, the agreement contained the phrase "shall support the accession of Turkey to the European Union." This was a crude *a priori* infringement on sovereignty. The Foundation Agreement, which was later rolled into the final text before the diplomatic charade in Switzerland, has quite rightly been described as a "marketing tool."[7]

Let us list the main partitionist elements of "Annan V" (apart from the obvious 1960 connection): first was the disproportionate power given to the minority, in the shape of the "common state" parliament's senate being composed of twenty-four Greek and Turkish Cypriots, respectively, meaning an effective veto by the minority. Second, important matters of state would, failing agreement, pass to a supreme court consisting (again, disproportionately) of three Greek and three Turkish Cypriots, respectively, and three non-Cypriots, thereby creating a protectorate in all but name, a protectorate where, into the bargain, Turkey had rights of intervention. Third, the majority of illegal settlers were to be allowed to remain, thus legalizing ethnic cleansing and manipulation. Fourth, only a proportion of refugees would have been able to reclaim their properties, and only on a staggered basis. In this connection, it is highly significant that the scheme would have done away with the right of Cypriots to appeal, as many have, to the European Court of Human Rights. Fifth, by introducing restrictive quotas based on ethnicity and religion, the plan violated the European Convention on Human Rights and the Treaty of Rome and subsequent law, in one fell swoop. Moreover, as mentioned in chapter 2 (pages 26-27), any form of discrimination, but particularly positive discrimination, is insulting and patronizing toward those it is allegedly intended to benefit, since they are treated like handicapped, weaker people, rather than as equals. Thus far, this seems to have gone over the heads of the Turkish Cypriots. Sixth, the Republic of Cyprus would have been dissolved and replaced by a loose confederation of two autonomous states. Given the previous history of the intercommunal negotiations, it would have been a miracle if the two divided bits would have agreed on everything, particularly given the influence of Turkey and its desire to enter the European Union. There would have been a period of considerable tension and a constitutional vacuum, with nothing to replace it. This would have given Turkey a pretext to occupy more of the island, which would have been easily achievable, since the plan allowed six thousand Turkish troops to remain for up to eight years, while the plan demilitarized Cyprus (apart, naturally, from the British bases).

As if the creation of second-class EU citizens (a veritable oxymoron), the legalization of illegality and the undermining of the EU's and the UN's very *raison d'être* were not enough, Britain tried to use the occasion to slip through expanded rights in the Sovereign Base Areas and adjacent waters. Yet more cynically, and at Turkey's behest (at least presentationally), the scheme revoked Cyprus's ratification of the 1936 Montreux Convention on navigation through the Straits, in line with Turkey's U.S.- and British-sponsored attempt to control the international waterway. It was, in short, a bizarre yet arrogant attempt to force a soon-to-be member state of the European Union to join as an emasculated shadow of a genuine member, ensure no future Greek or Cypriot opposition to Turkey's membership bid, and enhance Anglo-American domination in the Middle East.

Particularly insultingly, the full scheme, consisting of almost ten thousand pages, was only put onto the UN website at one minute to midnight on 23 April, the eve of the referendum in both free and occupied Cyprus. It contained, needless to say, many devils in the detail. Without even bothering to criticize the drafting of the referendum questions, it would have been bizarre to seriously expect anyone but an illegal settler to vote for the scheme (settlers from Turkey made up a significant percentage of the Turkish Cypriot vote).[8] Its rejection by some 76 percent of the Greek Cypriots and 35 percent of the Turkish Cypriots was predictable to any cool observer, particularly after President Papadopoulos mentioned many of the above points and advised against acceptance of the scheme. It is logical to assume that the illegal settlers influenced the positive vote in occupied Cyprus, and that without them, the genuine Turkish Cypriots might have also rejected the plan.

Conclusions

There were predictable howls of protest from frustrated diplomats and politicians, since the whole convoluted package had been presented as a panacea and a last chance for a solution, in a fashion that can only be described as puerile. Even Annan could not prevent himself from implying that the failure was the fault of the Greek Cypriots, while Hannay's book on how he failed ended with the subtly menacing and also supercilious words: "[I]t is difficult to see any solution straying far away from the Annan Plan which has been so widely [*sic*] endorsed. But if Turkey's candidature stalls or is blocked, it is not easy to be so sanguine."[9] These words are a sad epitaph for a career diplomat who was hauled out of retirement in order to present an image of impartiality. Yet the final words of his book betray, perhaps by default, that he was simply working in the interests of the Anglo-Americans, who were and are interested in maintaining and increasing their hold over the British bases and promoting the weakening of European cohesion, by bringing in Turkey, a new—and essentially Asian—member, before it is even remotely ready for membership.

The Cypriots and President Papadopoulos are to be thanked for having upheld, almost single-handedly and in the face of childish playground bullying tactics, both the integrity of their country and the democratic traditions of the European Union and of the United Nations, and checked, for a while at least, the slow slithering into the dishonesty and mediocrity of the diplomacy of the last few years: just as a dodgy sexed-up dossier was used to attack Iraq, so at the same time was a dodgy series of complicated and confusing documents considered necessary to reassert more control over Cyprus, and by extension, over the Middle East. President Papadopoulos saved Cyprus. The Cypriots were at least allowed to express their opinion, and are now in the strongest position they have been since the invasion, as the Turkish occupation becomes ever more ridiculous and the Turkish Cypriots are deprived of their European rights. The abject failure of the Annan scheme has underlined the need for a democratic and anti-partitionary solution to the island's problems, problems that have been dangerously coagulating for too long. Clearly, certain interests of other powers are simply detrimental to the interests of the people of Cyprus, and the only viable solution is a strictly European one, in line with past UN resolutions, that does not involve hidden geostrategic agendas, and above all, that does not seek to legitimize aggression, as the Annan Plan did. To really see what the Annan Plan was, one can consider a parallel scenario, and ask oneself what the reaction of the Turkish government would be if Hannay or the UN secretary general dropped into Ankara with a plan giving the 18 percent Kurdish population of Turkey some half the seats in the Senate, rights to block action in the Executive, and some 30 percent of the land.[10]

Nevertheless, if the plan had had more certainty and precise guarantees built into it, had not been such a blatant attempt to legitimize theft of property, and had not been so drastically amended at the last minute and then thrust on a whole population, giving it no time to read, digest, understand, consider, and evaluate the thousands of pages of the scheme, things might have turned out differently. The whole morality behind the scheme, but particularly its later stages, should be seen within the context of the web of lies and deceit that surrounded the illegal unilateral attack on Iraq.

We have looked so far in this book at the more historical aspects of the way in which partition has been introduced to Cyprus, in both a subtle and overt fashion, in order to preserve and further selfish external interests. We have seen how a small country with a small population has survived in adversity, even becoming a member of the European Union, and fending off the aggression perpetrated on pretences that are long past their sell-by date. We now, therefore, start to juxtapose and compare cases of partition, to see where Cyprus fits into the scheme of things and demonstrate the effects of partition in a comparative manner. In this way, we should be able to see Cyprus and the partition question in a clearer and broader context than has been the case so far.

CHAPTER FOUR

Juxtaposition and Comparison

No man is happy but by comparison.[1]

Introduction

The preceding chapters should have made one thing particularly obvious, almost by default: the fact that in Cyprus's thousands of years of recorded history, the phenomenon of territorial division of its people, in the modern meaning of the word "partition," is very recent, forced, and unnatural, the result of a cynical policy of manipulation by outside powers which titillated the darkest side of a minority of the inhabitants' characters, leading to radicalization and then to foreign invasion and illegal occupation. In fact, we have witnessed how Turkey has tried, and is still trying, to control Cyprus through a mistaken and dangerous policy of dividing its people, in order to control as much as it can of the island.

That Turkish policy is destabilizing and dangerous is obvious, given the fact that as late as 1963, when, as we have seen, the Turkish-sponsored auto-ghettoization began, the Turkish Cypriots had been living all over the island for several hundred years. There were Turkish Cypriot quarters in all the main cities. Of the villages, 392 were exclusively Greek Cypriot, 123 Turkish Cypriot, and 114 of mixed population, all three types of village being situated throughout the island. There was no logical reason for partition of any kind. Nor had there ever been.

Juxtaposing different situations is simple, since putting two or more things side by side is a straightforward process; but when one begins to try and find differences and similarities between two or more situations, difficulties arise, because no two situations are ever identical. This means that when one identifies an apparent similarity or difference shared by two situations, they have already been affected by the fact that the situations are themselves not exactly the same, and that one is, therefore, in fact looking at similarities or differences stemming from broader differences. In other words, and to put it more simply, and using religious differences as a common denominator of comparison, the Bosnian Serbs and the Bosniaks may be easily juxtaposed with the Greek Cypriots and Turkish Cypriots. But comparison becomes difficult, when one considers the fact that the Bosniaks were Slav Bogomils who had converted to Islam to avoid persecution by Roman Catholics and Christian Orthodox alike, while most of the Turkish Cypriots came to Cyprus after 1571, and were already Muslim. Then there is the fact that the Serb Bosnians and the Bosniaks spoke the same tongue, unlike the Christian and Muslim Cypriots. Yet more complicatedly, both the Croats and the Serbs claimed that the Bosniaks were Croats and Serbs, respectively. One encounters such distinctions before even trying to compare the case, for example, of Bosnia-Herzegovina with that of Cyprus. We write this simply to remind ourselves that in any of the comparisons which we shall make, exactitude is difficult, and that we shall, therefore, look for common factors which transcend different geographical and ethnic characteristics. Of these common factors, self-interested and intrusive foreign interference seems to be one of the main ones. We should bear in mind that we are dealing in this book with partition through foreign aggression.

Kosovo and Yugoslavia

The very word "Kosovo" triggers visions of the term "Balkanization" in its most pejorative sense. Certainly, comparing Kosovo to Cyprus is not easy, since the former was, and still is, legally part of a state, Serbia, while Cyprus is not part of a state. It is, however, unilateral aggression against a sovereign state that proves to be a common factor. In the case of Cyprus, military conquest has occasioned a continuing attempt to partition a sovereign state, and then to create a second one under occupation. In the case of Serbia, seventy-eight days of bombing led to a similar attempt to establish a new state, based on secession and the occupation of Kosovo, part of the sovereign state of Serbia.

Another parallel is the spurious claim that both attacks and occupations were to protect minority groups from ill-treatment by a majority, when their purpose was in fact strategic. In the case of the bombing of Serbia, NATO was able to coordinate its attack with the celebrations for its fiftieth birthday, the admission of three new members, and the concomitant macho-message to a Russia still emerging from the vagaries of over eighty years of socialist statism. In order to begin bombing, the United States had to change its policy: after U.S. envoy Robert Gelbard had labeled the Kosovo Liberation Army (KLA) as terrorists as recently as 23 February 1998,[2] U.S. envoy Richard Holbrooke then changed the tune, and openly fraternized with the KLA only four months later, confusing the Serbs, who had been presented with a blank check to root out the KLA. In October of that year, the KLA brutally rejected a U.S.-brokered solution, based on restoring provincial autonomy, with the moderate Ibrahim Rugova as president. The die was cast, and all that remained was for NATO to impose an unacceptable condition on Serbia, namely, that Serbia "allow NATO to use Serbia as part of the NATO organisation."[3] This unacceptable infringement of sovereignty was paralleled in 1914 by Austria's demand that its police have a free reign in Serbia to find the assassin of Archduke Franz Ferdinand and his wife Sophie.

To describe eleven weeks of bombing as "humanitarian intervention" was simply grotesque, particularly since the prime objective was to get NATO into Kosovo, rather than to avert a human disaster.[4] According to one expert, who was himself a NATO war planner, the "substantive political objective of averting civil war had to yield precedence to the time-bound public relations objective, with its deadline of NATO's birthday."[5]

In the case of Cyprus, we find a similar measure of hypocrisy and double standards, since the Turkish claim that their armed forces intervened to protect their minority was almost immediately shown to be false: when the so-called "Sampson coup" took place, the Turkish Cypriots were left alone. According to the commander of British Forces Near East,

> Turkey . . . was fast talking herself into military intervention to protect the allegedly beleaguered Turkish Cypriot community. That they were in fact in no danger and that Turkey had no genuine pretext for military intervention is well illustrated by Mr. Olver's [British high commissioner, Nicosia] telegram.[6]

It was only as the Cypriot armed forces, following the reestablishment of constitutional order, began to resist the Turkish attack that intercommunal tensions rose, understandably, given the massiveness of the invasion and ejection of Greek Cypriots from their homes, accompanied by hundreds of Greek Cypriot civilian deaths.

Another parallel one can draw relates to the people affected by the military aggression. In the case of Serbia, over one hundred thousand Serbs were forced to leave Kosovo, as internally displaced refugees, while the same happened in Cyprus, with the number twice as high.

Bosnia-Herzegovina and Cyprus are also similar, in that neither had easily definable homogenously settled areas, but, rather, mixed populations spread over the former Yugoslav republic and island, respectively. Demographic dispersion was the order of the day, and still would be, were it not for the manic quest for partition, which not only causes immense suffering but also leads to future conflict. In this connection, the Dayton Accords, which created more future problems than they solved, can be likened to the Annan Plan, namely, a hidden partition agreement.

At a more "macro" Balkan level, one can draw a tentative, but nevertheless interesting parallel between the invasion and occupation of Cyprus and the partitioning of Yugoslavia by Germany, Italy, and Bulgaria in World War II. It is perhaps to be bewailed that Turkey considered it necessary to behave in such a wartime German-Italian-Bulgarian fashion thirty years after the ending of such behavior in Europe. It would have been wiser to heed the United Nations, something that we shall discuss later in this chapter.

A final parallel is, of course, the fact that both Cyprus and the Balkans have historically been victims of the strategic ambitions and machinations of foreign powers, in particular of the Ottoman Empire, and that this tendency to interfere and divide is still with us today, whatever the lip-service paid to international law. The current partition of Bosnia Herzegovina is a good example of how partition is used to expediently paper over cracks, without solving the nub of a problem. For example, only a small proportion of the Serbs from

(Bosnian) Krajina have returned to their homes, memories of their expulsion in 1991–95 combining with those of the wartime slaughter of 750,000 of their ancestors by the Croat Ustashe allies of Nazi Germany. As one expert writes, "Self-determination should be concerned primarily with people, not territory."[7] Partition can in fact be the very antithesis of genuine self-determination, since, as we have seen, it is inevitably the result of territorial and strategic machinations by competing foreign powers, in tandem with minority quisling politicopaths.

The Indian Connection

India, a huge and diverse subcontinent, and Cyprus, a small Mediterranean island, do not lend themselves to immediate comparison. Yet there are some connections, the most obvious being that Lord Radcliffe, charged with partitioning India in 1947, was also responsible for drawing up constitutional proposals for Cyprus in 1956. After World War II, it was generally expected that Cyprus, along with India and Burma, would be given up by the British. As we have seen, however, Cyprus bucked the trend, with unfortunate consequences which would, however, manifest themselves soon after the island's eventual qualified independence. The case of India was catastrophic, showing *par excellence* the perils of partition.[8] The partition of India into India and Pakistan caused untold problems. First was the latter's separation into two pieces, some two thousand kilometers apart. Second was the subdivision of old territories such as the Punjab and Bengal. The British appeared obsessed by the idea of division by religion, whether Muslim (which they tended to favor, as in Cyprus), Hindu, or Sikh. Never mind that peoples had shared the same territory and language for centuries. The British ensured that religion would become a dividing factor for the future. It goes without saying that, just as the British defined the differences, as they did in Cyprus, so did they create problems, problems that are still with us. As one expert has written, a "divide and rule" policy was followed, using map drawings, census operations, and notions of separate electorates.[9] Just as the 1960 settlement in Cyprus left the crucial area of municipalities undone, so did the British leave India with a certain measure of indecent haste, months earlier than previously announced,[10] leaving, in particular, the question of Kashmir to be thrashed out between mutually hostile elites, a hostility it had itself nurtured. The results were wars in 1948 and 1965 between India and Pakistan over Kashmir. In 1948, around one million people were killed and around ten million displaced, a tragedy of almost surrealistic proportions. British "administrative interference" much earlier also led to problems between the new Pakistan and Afghanistan, simply because the British had created an arbitrary border in 1893 dividing the Pashtun people. At the time of writing, there are enormous problems on that very border.

To rub salt into the wounds created by the cancer of partition, East Pakistan seceded with Indian military help in 1971, renaming itself Bangladesh. The results of the partition of India are still with us today, and bode badly for the future, given the unresolved Kashmir problem, terrorist attacks in India and Pakistan, occasional threats of war between the two nuclear powers, and instability in Pakistan that has even led to it exporting nuclear technology and housing all manner of Muslim extremists, many from Afghanistan.

Before we end this sorry section, let us remember that even without formal partition plans, as *per* India, irresponsible and selfish behavior *per se* can lead to terrible strife and divisiveness. The most obvious case within the Indian context is that of the Hindu Tamils in Sri Lanka, brought into predominantly Buddhist Ceylon by the British from the south of India during the colonial era to work on the tea plantations. The result was and is a vicious civil war of attrition that has led to atrocities for years, and continues to trouble the island. Even with the apparent defeat of the "Tamil Tigers," the bitterness, and thus future problems, remain. Although another island, Ireland, has been spared serious strife for a few years, it is there that we now turn, to further demonstrate the perils of partition.

Ireland

An immediate connection with Cyprus is that both are islands that, following conquest, were forcefully settled by alien peoples of antagonistic religious persuasions. Both occurred at around the same time, toward the end of the sixteenth century and then, more spasmodically, later. One big difference is that the illegal settlement of 160,000 Anatolians in Cyprus from 1974 on has not been replicated in the bit of Ireland that is still under British rule, perhaps because the descendants of those settlers still outnumber the local inhabitants. In the case of Cyprus, on the other hand, the aggressor decided to try and create an (illegal) *fait accompli* by bringing in outsiders, something that had not been done for four hundred years.

To understand the perils of partition in the case of Ireland, and then to seek parallels with Cyprus, we need to turn back to at least 1921, when the English partitioned Ireland. Following immense internal strife and a large measure of English cruelty, London in the end offered partition, by carving off the largest part of the province of Ulster. Not only did this mark the beginning of an illogical and unnatural division of the island based, at the time, on religion, but it also even involved fracturing Ulster, an ancient kingdom in its own right. Here, the most obvious parallel with Cyprus is the "divide, quit, but keep" syndrome, in the shape of the British Sovereign Territories. Essentially, Britain was not prepared to leave completely and let the inhabitants manage their own affairs, but instead wished to maintain some sort of control lever. In the case of Ireland, the excuse was that in part of Ireland there was a Protestant majority, while in the case of Cyprus, military strategy was the excuse, plus the fact that Britain did not trust the Cypriots themselves to "stick with the West" in the Cold War: Cyprus's strongest political party was Marxist-oriented and thus separated religion from the state. Britain therefore used the religious ploy, to combat any mentality that united Greek- and

Turkish-speaking Christians and Muslims, respectively. In this connection, we should recall that several champions of Irish unity, such as Charles Parnell, were minority Protestants. Such people, moderates to the core, were dangerous to the promoters of division.

Another interesting parallel is the cynical use of territory as a bargaining chip. Thus, Britain offered to free Cyprus in 1915 if Greece entered the Great War, while in 1940, the Churchill government made a similar offer to unite Ireland if it joined Britain against Germany. But the Irish leader, Eamon de Valera, saw nothing to be gained by involvement in violence and remained neutral, like Sweden, the Netherlands, Spain, and Portugal. The Swedes, in particular, had long come to terms with their military Carl Gustavian days, while the Dutch had never had designs in Europe. Similarly, the Irish had never displayed hegemonistic tendencies, but rather had themselves been subject to the unwelcome hegemonistic attentions of one or more larger powers, just like Cyprus. In this connection, in its extreme keenness to see the perilously partitionist Annan Plan introduced, Britain even offered almost half the area of the SBA's to the new Cyprus that would have allegedly emerged from the plan.

A similarity between Cyprus and Ireland is that both have been the object of military action to maintain and promote partition, even if the manner of the arrival of troops was not the same. A major difference is that a UN peacekeeping force never came to Ireland.

Here, we must point out some major differences between Cyprus's and Ireland's predicaments. First, Ireland's division is at least internationally recognized, while neither the occupation nor the partition of Cyprus is. Turkey's policy has always been, and still is, to achieve at least partition and, if possible, to use this to ultimately gain control of the whole island. Second, the atavistic and near tribal religious and cultural differences between the Protestant "Orangemen" and the Roman Catholic Republican Irish are far more deep-seated than in Cyprus. Despite the different religions in Cyprus, religious fanaticism has never been an issue, although the colonial power, together with Turkey, certainly tried to exploit divisions, managing to instill a strong sense of Turkish nationalism among the Turkish-speaking Muslims that had not been a serious factor before the 1950s.

Although the division of Ireland is currently not causing any overt strife, it should be remembered that behind the whole current delicate arrangement of the so-called Good Friday Agreements lies a complicated historical myriad of nationalism, religion, and atavism that cannot simply disappear overnight at the waving of a magic wand. The continuing presence of the British armed forces speaks quiet volumes. Just as few predicted the break-up of Yugoslavia before the fall of the Berlin Wall, so no one dares to be so negative as to predict further major strife in Ulster. It would be politically incorrect. Yet who, with his hand on his heart, could say that the island of Ireland will still be divided in thirty years? And if it is reunited, will it be through further strife or by the democratic will of the majority, a will that has not been allowed to manifest itself in Cyprus? When the Roman Catholic population of Ulster becomes a serious electoral threat to the Protestant Unionist parties ("Disunionist" being perhaps a more apposite term), then we can expect to see further strife, accompanied by all manner of electoral boundary machinations and administrative chicanery, unless Dublin and London really are able to achieve final unification of one of England's earliest colonial exploits.

Demographic Ripple Effect

We have seen how one of the multifarious methods of partitioning countries is through importing large groups of alien people into once homogenous areas. At the time this happens, the intention may be purely practical. For example, Britain's motives in importing around one million Tamils into Ceylon (see above, page 49) in the nineteenth century were essentially commercial. It is unlikely that the colonial businessmen were thinking of dividing the population or creating future strife, so often a prelude to attempts at partition. The motive was essentially short- and medium-term profit, although, as we see today, the damage was long-term. Cyprus contrasts vividly with this, since the 160,000 illegal Anatolian settlers have been brought in, not to help profits, but to artificially change the natural demographic balance of the island and to further *de facto* partition, with the childishly obvious objective of creating a *fait accompli*, thus rendering a just and balanced settlement of the issues at stake increasingly difficult, in terms of international legal and moral norms, particularly European ones. This explains why Turkey, knowing that its legal legs are weak, is always hankering for a political rather than a legal solution. As the Foreign Office wrote, "In short what the Greeks want is a legal settlement while the Turks want a political one."[11] Although the comment involved the Turkish claims to Greek Aegean territory, it applies equally to Cyprus, indeed, all the more so, since Turkey is in direct breach of international law, whereas in the case of its Aegean claims, it has not actually permanently occupied any of the islets that it claims or set up oil-drilling stations within Greek maritime limits, merely probing and provoking, often when it wishes to up the stakes on Cyprus. It is presumably aware, as the FCO has stated, that its Aegean case is weak.[12] Thus, we see here the ripple effect of Turkey's occupation and demographic manipulation of a sovereign state. The more illegal salt that Turkey rubs into the wound it has created, the more this connects to its claims on the territory of another country (Greece), particularly in terms of a so-called political solution. Within the context of Cyprus and Turkish claims on Greek territory, "political" really means "non-legal" at best and "illegal" at worst. As we have seen, Turkey has always been suspicious of the UN, to the extent of flouting its resolutions, as we shall see in the following chapter. And since we are juxtaposing and comparing in this chapter, let us now take a brief but piercing look at the above-mentioned Galo Plaza Report of 1965, perhaps the most sensible UN effort to solve the problem, bearing in mind the now null and void Annan Plan.

Unacceptable Separation

On 26 March 1965, UN mediator Galo Plaza submitted his report on Cyprus to the UN secretary general. In his most telling and pertinent statement, he noted that,

> In the first place, the separation of the communities is utterly unacceptable to the majority community of Cyprus and on present indications could not be imposed except by force . . . It would seem to require a compulsory movement of the people concerned—many thousands on both sides—contrary to all the enlightened principles of the present time, including those set forth in the Universal Declaration of Human Rights. . . . Such a state of affairs would constitute a lasting, if not permanent, cause of discontent and unrest.

The report's main suggestions were that Cyprus exclude *enosis,* be demilitarized and neutral, exclude partition, not maintain the same privileges for the Turkish Cypriots as in the 1960 arrangements (but grant them additional and exceptional protection), that the UN should guarantee any agreed settlement, and that the Cypriots should vote on any settlement totally, and not partially.

As mentioned above, Turkey was smarting from the involvement of the UN, but in particular from the latter's recognition of the legitimate government, and rejected the report. The Turkish Cypriots had imposed isolation on themselves and were completely dependent on, and influenced by, Turkey.[13] Viewed with the benefit of hindsight, it is clearly unfortunate that Turkey and the Turkish Cypriots did not jump at the opportunity of at least getting the ball rolling, even on the basic principle that "jaw-jaw" is better than "war-war."

In advising against the idea of federation, Galo Plaza was clearly looking at the term as signifying physical and territorial separation. We need to be extremely careful here, since a functional federation can also work without separating vital functions of state, or involving the constitutional separation of territories and people. We need only to turn to Germany or the United States to understand this. It is, rather, the nature of a particular federation which is germane. Ankara was clearly exploiting the term to signify a form of partition, or at least a step towards partition. Any "federation" imposed from outside could be tantamount to partition, or at least interpreted as such, in the absence of intercommunal negotiations to arrive at a mutually agreed constitutional settlement. In line with UN resolutions, the objective is an independent, nonaligned, and bicommunal federation, a concept to which President Makarios subscribed, albeit with some soul-searching, in 1977. We shall turn to this in the final chapter, when we look at the European solution. Thus far, we are left with the intriguing thought that Cyprus is far more a case of straightforward aggression and occupation, as in Yugoslavia and Greece in World War II, than of simple agreed partition, as in the case of Czechoslovakia.

Conclusions

Although it may be true that good fences make good neighbors, this only really applies at the level of people's properties, where a well-built—and agreed—wall clarifies a boundary, thereby nipping potential disputes in the bud. But this well-worn and rather trite maxim begins to lose meaning once we reach the level of political, particularly geopolitical, borders. The so-called Iron Curtain, for example, was one of the most effective borders on Earth, but hardly contributed to good-neighborliness, even between people of similar historical development and culture, such as the Germans. Their political elites were at loggerheads, even to the extent of shooting dead those trying to escape from East to West. The crucial point here is that the border was imposed on Germany and thus came to represent tension and potential conflict. Similarly, the borders imposed on Germany after the Great War were in many cases artificial, and a major cause of World War II. We can, then, suggest that it is more pertinent, particularly in the case of Cyprus, to stipulate that *bad* fences make *bad* neighbors, not only at the territorial but also at the constitutional level. Here we are, of course, referring to the inequalities of the ethnically conceived 1960 arrangement, while today we are referring to a fence imposed by armed force that artificially induces feelings of mutual hostility by detracting from and bedeviling clear communication. Such an imposed situation can fester and become putrid, all the more so when such huge swaths of the population have been uprooted. About 40 percent of the Greek Cypriot population were torn from their land. To try and understand such a trauma, it is as if, proportionately at least, some 120 million Americans were forced to leave their lands on the east coast, and go west. The analogy may be crude, but still helps us to grasp the scope of the problem. We also see from history that actions even thousands of years ago can still have repercussions today. Although this is a truism, it is one often ignored by the promoters of selfish and short-term strategies. The Romans, for example, declared Greece independent of Macedonia because it suited them, thus creating future disputes that bedevil the Hellenic world to this day. What transpires from even a brief look at partition is that one of its central characteristics is demographic manipulation.

On a related tack, and particularly relevant to Cyprus, we have plenty of examples of different minorities living happily in a "majority" country. Take the Turkish-speaking Muslim populations of Thrace, Rhodes, and Kos, generally far happier as EU citizens and Greek nationals than the beleaguered Turkish Cypriots, who have been swamped by alien Anatolians with different customs. We shall devote a section to them later. Take the German-speakers of Eupen and Malmédy, happy as Belgian citizens and protected by Belgian and European law. The same is the case for the German speakers of the Alto Adige in Italy, who are happy Italian citizens attending their German-speaking schools. But the same is not the case for the ill-treated Kurds of Turkey, for the simple reason that they do not have equal rights. The Turkish government could well take a leaf out of Makarios's book and bravely agree to a functional bicommunal solution, thus allowing Turkish Cypriots EU rights. This is clearly a case of double standards. On the one hand, Turkey is promoting partition in Cyprus, while denying even a form of federation to its Kurdish brothers. The histories of the Muslim Cypriots and the Kurds of Turkey may not be the same, but the principles involved are similar. There is an element of ingratitude on the part of Turkey, since the Kurdish role in the military was vital in creating modern Turkey.

The very idea of the EU is of course intrinsically anti-partitionist, and we shall deal with this aspect later. As we begin to see the dangers of the extremism, and of the extreme actions, that have led to the occupation of an EU member state, we see that partition is a clumsy, neo-tribal pseudo-solution, characterized by casuistic, shallow, and imprecise PR language, creating both underlying tension and future problems. On that note, we now move towards the nub of this book, by considering the European, legal, moral, economic, political, and practical arguments against partition.

CHAPTER FIVE

Dismembering Dismemberment Arguments

Borders are scratched across the hearts of men
By strangers with a calm judicial pen.[1]

Introduction

In this chapter, we shall first spell out some arguments used in favor of partition, and then expose the humbug. Then we shall discuss consecutively the above-mentioned European, legal, moral, economic, political, and practical arguments against partition and therefore in favor of genuine reunification of the Cypriot state, its economy, its society, and its institutions, in favor of integrated coexistence. We have seen how foreign interference and extremism unnaturally bedeviled and ruptured the benign coexistence of the people of Cyprus in the fifties, coexistence that had subsisted for hundreds of years and which should be allowed to return unfettered in the future. We have seen how distasteful partition can be, and how it is often the result of expediency, selfish and greedy national interests, and even laziness, incompetence and, therefore, lack of precision, the latter being a catch-all human trait that can lead to strife and war. Let us recall how Galo Plaza dismissed the idea of separation of the communities as contrary to all enlightened principles, including those set forth in the Universal Declaration of Human Rights, that brave document that has been so battered by the extremists of international relations. We begin at the universal, in other words, the UN, level.

Utilitarian Escape

The utilitarian ideas of "the end justifies the means" and of "the greatest happiness for the greatest number" are too well-known to require extensive comment. Suffice to say that in regard to partition, the utilitarian approach tends to lead to the biggest unhappiness for the minority, thereby creating resentment. The typical argument for partition reads as follows: when an ethnic war is far advanced, partition is probably the most humane form of intervention, because it attempts to achieve through negotiation what would otherwise be achieved through fighting; it circumvents the conflict and saves lives. It might even save a country from disappearing altogether, because an impartial intervener will attempt to secure the rights of each contending ethnic group, whereas in war, the stronger groups might oust the weaker ones. Therefore, the ideal strategy is to intervene and take partition to its logical conclusion by dividing the country along its communal battle lines and helping to make the resulting territories ethnically homogenous through organized population transfers. This, so the argument runs, will ensure that partition is more than a temporary means of containing conflict. Less thorough partitions, however, can still be a lasting means of containment.[2]

Generally, this argument is simplistic and Manichean in thinking, since it starts out by assuming a "far advanced" ethnic war, whereas often there is nothing of the sort. Matters are usually far more complex and cannot be conveniently packaged to suit the partition argument. In the case of Cyprus, there was an easy relationship for hundreds of years between the two main communities, and then some externally provoked measures led to some rioting, but certainly not an ethnic war, let alone a far advanced one. As to whether it circumvents conflict, partition can actually do the opposite, simply giving it a more institutional and long-term form. One look at Ireland, but especially Palestine and India, tell us the dangers of partition, which led to mass killings. Matters, moreover, are never simple demographically, even in areas which are mainly homogenous. There are inevitably isolated groups, which buck the trend of "racial, religious or cultural homogeneity," a trend which is in any case primitively racist in conception. One academic supporter of partition implies, in the case of Cyprus, that Turkey's invasion saved thousands of lives.[3] This is fantasy and wishful thinking: the British intelligence report of the invasion actually stated that the Turkish Cypriots were in no danger and that Turkey had no genuine pretext for military intervention.[4] The "life-saving" argument is intellectually inadequate, as it depends on a hypothesis, namely, that there would be mass killing without partition, already shown to be nonsense in the case of Cyprus. On the contrary, the invasion and forced splitting of Cyprus led to the deaths of over three thousand, killed mainly by the Turkish army, plus a number of missing Greek Cypriots, currently fourteen hundred. As we have seen, the rioting of 1958 and 1963 was Turkish-provoked, and as such was simply part of Turkey's unnatural partition strategy.

The dangers of expedient argumentation can be seen in the occasional use of postwar Franco-German reconciliation over Alsace and Lorraine to justify partitioning Cyprus. In a 1997 article on Cyprus, we read:

> If an agreement on a federal state cannot be reached, it may be time to contemplate formal partition . . . Once the borders are made clear and their international status is settled, the two sides in the Cyprus conflict, like France and Germany before them, could get on with reconciliation, economic interaction and a stable peace.[5]

By comparing Cyprus with France and Germany, the writer is ignoring the fact that Cyprus is a single country, while France and Germany are two entirely separate entities. Historically, France and Germany bear little, if any, comparison with Cyprus. Unlike Cyprus, France and the Holy Roman Empire, and then Germany, had quarreled over Alsace and Lorraine for centuries. It is precisely this kind of simplistic, uninformed, and crooked thinking that has bedeviled Cyprus for too long.

The case of Palestine is another example of the evil that partition can bring. The declaration of the state of Israel almost immediately led to a form of twisted self-partition and annexation combined, involving the expulsion of some 750,000 innocent Palestinians from their ancestral lands (and that of a large number of Jews from Arab countries). But there was no corresponding creation of a state of Palestine, as called for by a UN resolution partitioning Palestine (but bickered over by the Security Council). To rub salt into the illegal wound, Zionist fanatics then murdered the moderate UN mediator Count Bernadotte. He had been trying to modify the UN partition plan by ensuring the return with compensation of those uprooted (mainly Palestinians) and making Jerusalem an international city. Thus began one of the most intractable international relations problems the world has ever known, the result of a skewed partition and its institutionalization. It is no exaggeration to say that hundreds of thousands of innocent people have been killed as a result of Bernadotte's brutal murder, somewhat ironic in a twisted way, since, as head of the Swedish Red Cross, he had saved thousands of Jews from concentration camps in World War II by negotiating directly with Heinrich Himmler. His reward was bitter.

The more extreme a supporter of Zionism one is, the more one tends to support both the Protestants of Ulster and the Turkish occupiers of Cyprus, with a common factor being that the respective partitions have depended, and still depend on, overwhelming military force.[6] Certainly, the cases of the fates of Palestine and Cyprus are linked by, first, the fact that both Israel and Turkey are illegally occupying territory, and second, that both countries have expelled large numbers of people and replaced them with illegal settlers. Only Turkey recognizes the "TRNC," while most countries reject Israel's annexation of East Jerusalem and of the Golan Heights.[7] It is, then, hardly surprising that one academic partition-monger ends his piece favoring the divisions of Ireland, India, Palestine, and Cyprus with the words:

> Similarly, the international community should stop pressing winners of ethnic wars to take back refugees of the other side, and should stop pushing refugees to return when they fear for their lives if they do. After an ethnic war, repatriating any substantial number of refugees back to territory held by the other group risks making control of that territory once again uncertain, thus recreating the same security dilemma that helped escalate the conflict in the first place.[8]

If this apparent argument is taken to its logical conclusion, it is stating that illegal conquest and ethnic cleansing are legitimate. But worst of all, the author avoids the obvious question of illegal immigration into conquered territory. He takes us back to the Dark Ages and the invasion of Attila's Huns. Many partition-mongers also tend to indulge in hegemonolinguistic humbuggery and twisted euphemisms: they might, for example, refer to occupied territory as "disputed" and the building of illegal settlements as "unhelpful." This is akin to describing genocide as "civil war" (as the Turkish government has in the case of the mass massacres of Armenians), rape as "naughty," murder as "collateral damage," torture flights as "extraordinary renditions," and illegal immigrants as "seasonal workers" (viz. occupied Cyprus). At any rate, we see how arguments in favor of partition tend to be close to justifying the original crime that started a problem.

One political science theoretician supports "continued partition in the short term,"[9] apparently naively and blissfully unaware of the harsh reality that his short-term and expedient argument plays into the hands of the illegal and anti-European partitionist policy that Turkey has pursued to date. A real expert puts him in his place: "Too frequently, partition was embraced as a temporary expedient which invariably became a permanent condition whereby national and/or ethnic groups were tragically separated by artificial divisions."[10] In contrast to this thoughtfulness and common sense, the writer even advocates recognizing occupied Cyprus, so that "both 'North and South Cyprus' will become [*sic*] de facto united as members of the EU."[11] This comes close to applauding Turkish aggression and sends a very irresponsible signal to other would-be aggressors and extremists the world over. Predictably, as with so many supporters of partition (and of Annan V), he also connects his arguments to Turkey's putative EU membership, which he clearly supports. Simply put, he seems to be arguing that if you wish to join the EU, the formula is simple: invade a country, carve off one third of its territory, throw out its inhabitants without compensation, replace them with illegal settlers, get the invaded territory recognized, and, before you know it, the EU will welcome you into their bosom. The European argument, to which we now turn, is perhaps the strongest rebuff to partition-mongering, since its very ethos is antithetical to the concept of partition (if we can even grace the word with the term "concept").

The European Solution

The most obvious argument against any form of partition, both generally and in the case of Cyprus, is the example of the European Union, the very *raison d'être* of which is to bring countries and people together. It is quintessentially centripetal economically and politically, however slow the integration process may be and whatever the occasional vicissitudes. In contrast to European norms, from the very beginning of the modern state of Cyprus, its constitution institutionalized communal dualism in all spheres of government, rather than allow integration of the two ethnic groups,[12] thus creating a future institutional dichotomy in Cyprus's relationship with the EEC and then EU. Despite some almost insurmountable hurdles, Cyprus is now nevertheless a member of the club and doing its best to support the European ideal. The stronger and more developed that EU law becomes, the less the tendency for small groups to seek increased autonomy. French- and Dutch-speaking Belgians will never separate, whatever their occasional spats, just as Belgium's German-speakers are content. As the European Communities developed in the sixties, so the Alto Adige problem fizzled out. Although there are still problems with a small section of activist Basques in Spain and, to a lesser extent, with the Catalans and Galicians, the EU, with its developing law, acts as a counterweight to extreme secessionist tendencies and even accommodates them within unity. In the case of Scotland, one can also pose the legitimate argument that if Britain were more *communautaire* politically and economically, a large portion of the Scottish people might be less inclined to go their own way. The case of Ulster is yet more pertinent. Had Britain and Ireland been founding members of the EEC, then the *acquis* would slowly but surely have at least detracted from the division of Ireland, bringing, if not rapid reunification, then, at least, more mutual respect and less extremism.

The European Union does indeed act as a healing balm in many a dispute, and even where a dispute may not have yet been totally solved, the slowly developing European identity makes the mere thought of military threats from one member toward another an impossibility, if not a childish absurdity. Such is the case, for example, with the Eems-Dollard estuary between Germany and the Netherlands. There is in fact no agreed maritime border between the two countries. But the European spirit prevails. There are no invasion threats from either side. At the end of the last war, before the European spirit of reconciliation began to make itself felt, the Netherlands laid claim to 1,750 square kilometers of Germany, managing to be given 70, with a population of 10,000. Following the signing of the Treaty of Rome and the growing spirit of peace and reconciliation, the annexation began to stick out like a sore thumb, and the Netherlands returned the territory in 1963. The current unnatural cleavage in Cyprus contrasts vividly with the idea of Europe: it is not merely a primitive anachronism, but an affront to modern European civilization and legal norms. Since the Maastricht agreement, with its economic, social, and defense and foreign policy components, the European project has continued, slowly but nevertheless inexorably, with the prospect of a proper constitution now looking more possible than ever, however slowly the European tortoise ambles along. One of the worst aspects of Cyprus's situation is that the Turkish Cypriots are being denied their European rights through the actions of an alien power which not only is keeping Cyprus artificially divided but whose actions are also an affront to the traditions, norms, and principles of the European Union. Any suggested solution that detracts from the *acquis* and from European law in general weakens the process of European integration as well as the likelihood of a federal solution to Cyprus's problems. By federal, we mean, of course, a federation based on European norms and not a slithery semantic pseudo-panacea that could lead to another artificial and dependent statelet, further partition, tension, and a weakening of the functioning of European institutions.

A great deal of emotional and uninformed humbug is used, often by crypto-nationalists, to undermine the idea of a united Europe. The reality is that through the EU concept of subsidiarity, a problem will be dealt with at member-state level, if it can be, and only at supra-national level if it is too big and/or complex to be dealt with by an individual member. Since Cyprus is occupied by a country with a population about eighty times that of its own, and with NATO's second largest army, it is obvious that only the EU as a whole can involve itself in a solution, rather than avoid the issue and thereby weaken itself.

In the case of Cyprus, it is clear that genuine reunification can only come about through the *acquis communautaire* which, unlike the divisive ethno-religious "solutions" periodically thrust on the island, will ensure no discrimination, treating all Cypriots as equal and guaranteeing the rights of the individual. One of the major weaknesses of the Annan Plan was the huge number of derogations from EU law which undermined the three most basic legal elements of the European Union, namely, freedom of movement of people, goods, and capital. As the European Court of Justice increases its responsibilities (see its landmark judgment below, page 67), it will become increasingly difficult to discriminate against groups or individuals. The 1960 arrangement of Cyprus is, as it stands, both a quasi-legal nightmare and a serious obstacle to a comprehensive solution. It requires radical surgery, rather than the cosmetic tinkering that we have witnessed to date. To find a solution before the *acquis communautaire* can be applied to the whole island is extremely difficult, since the 1960 treaties themselves are contrary not only to the spirit of the UN Charter but also to the principles of the EU. A solution, therefore, needs to be worked out in tandem with the EU and the Cypriots directly, while Britain, Greece, and Turkey sort out among themselves how to divest themselves of the mess caused by the 1960 arrangement. It is worth considering how happy the Turkish Cypriots would be, if they had the same rights and living conditions as the Muslims of Rhodes and Kos, who have the same European rights as the rest of the population of Greece. Let us now consider the legal situation, a veritable minefield of utilitarian and expedient debate, and try and find some precision, with the purpose of showing how international law is very much on the side of the Republic of Cyprus.

Obscuring Illegality

The core factor in the argument against separation of communities is the authority of the United Nations, so often the whipping boy of international relations, a somewhat unfair situation if one realizes that it merely represents the policies of the five permanent members of the Security Council (SC), and that to attack the UN is really the same as attacking the states which created it. It is nevertheless largely thanks to the UN and the way in which it balances sometimes mutually hostile states in the Security Council, that compromises can be found that can dampen military adventurism. Thus, it was the UN that helped to prevent a Turkish invasion in 1963/64, with SC Resolution 186 of 4 March 1964 that authorized the secretary general to reach a settlement in accordance with the UN Charter, place peacekeeping forces in Cyprus, appoint a mediator, and reaffirm the sovereignty of Cyprus. To considerable Turkish irritation, the resolution asked the government of Cyprus, which "has the responsibility for the maintenance and restoration of law and order, to take all additional measures necessary to stop violence and bloodshed in Cyprus." Thus, no official recognition whatsoever was afforded to the Turkish- or

Greek-Cypriot community, as separate entities. It was only Turkey that continued to push for separation, thumbing their noses at the UN. Since then, there have been numerous resolutions calling for the territorial integrity of Cyprus to be respected and for the withdrawal of foreign forces. It is significant that President Makarios (see above, page 35) agreed to an independent, non-aligned and bicommunal federal republic, thus yielding a great deal, both psychologically and in practical terms, to the Turkish Cypriots. It is equally significant that in so doing he called Turkey's bluff, since its intransigence continued. The new flexibility of the Cypriot government was reflected in particular in UN Resolution 1189 of 28 June 1998, which called for two politically equal communities in a bicommunal and bizonal federation. Here, the Turkish government simply decided to interpret the phrase "politically equal" as "politically separate," and "federation" as "confederation." Legally, however, it is clear that a federation, particularly one with a single sovereignty and international personality, as stipulated for Cyprus in various UN resolutions, ranks as equal to a unitary state.[13] Imprecise and weasel phrases like "loose federation" merely muddy the waters. The point is that any federation must be functional. Annan V was laden with obfuscatory and loose language that detracted from precision and that could have been interpreted by the partitionist-minded Turkish government and their supporters as simply a further stage towards partition, and possibly worse. It was the lack of watertight security guarantees that occasioned Russia to reject a Security Council resolution purporting to strengthen those guarantees. To avoid doubt about what is a proper legal solution, President Demetris Christofias made matters clear in his statement on 3 September 2008 on the launch of the intercommunal negotiations:

> A solution based on a bizonal, bicomunal federation was a major concession made by President Makarios in 1977, and due credit should be given to this concession. I wish to be clear from the beginning of the present negotiations: With this concession [bizonal, bicommunal federation], the Greek Cypriot side has exhausted its limits and cannot go any further. Neither confederation nor any partnership of two states through "virgin birth" can be accepted.[14]

President Christofias had stated in his inaugural address on 28 February 2008 and emphasized several times since that

> The federal, bizonal, bicomunal Republic of Cyprus must have one single sovereignty and international personality and one single citizenship. The solution must be based on the United Nations resolutions on Cyprus and be compatible with international and EU law, as well as with international conventions on human rights.

Since the collapse of the post-World War II order in Europe following the tearing down of the Berlin Wall, there has been an increasing lack of precision and an increase in express semantic ambiguity in international legal argumentation. This has been accompanied by legally questionable and simply illegal international violence, such as the bombing of Serbia and the invasion of Iraq. While on the one hand a former NATO war planner makes clear that the bombing of Serbia was not sanctioned by the UN (it therefore breached the UN Charter) and that its main purpose was to reinvent NATO as a worldwide policeman and use it as a tool of a new U.S.-inspired unilateral strategy based on a moralistic approach,[15] on the other, an international lawyer's views provide a perfect example of how to avoid precision and undermine international law. The latter ended an article on the Rambouillet Conference on Kosovo with the somewhat obfuscatory sentence:

> The connection of the legal justification of humanitarian action with the aim of achieving FRY/Serb acceptance of the Rambouillet package in its entirety, if it is maintained, would represent an innovative but justifiable extension of international law.[16]

One could well replace the word "extension" with "undermining," given the results of the illegal action to date. Publication of the article happened to coincide with the start of the bombing. The author also happened to have acted as a legal adviser to the Kosovo delegation at Rambouillet (which only represented the Albanians). In his article, he chose not to dwell on the illegality of the whole affair. Since the author tries to insiduously justify illegality, then by the same token, we ourselves need have no qualms in observing that the promoters of partition rely on legal ambiguity and even a form of low-level intellectual anarchy. The seventeenth-century Dutch legal theorist Hugo Grotius must be turning in his grave, and that is not said humorously. The whole story of the invasion of Iraq is even more relevant to our argument here, particularly since it coincides with the Annan negotiations. The invasion led to a *de facto* division of the country that has contributed to further destabilization of an already unstable Middle East. The fact that the sub-intellectual semantic chicanery accompanied outright lying about the reasons for attacking a sovereign state was no accident. Being economical with the truth is a factor that goes hand in hand with the promoters of partition in Cyprus. It explains the tendency by Turkey, the United States, and Britain to stress that a political rather than a legal solution needs to be found. Here, we can equate the word "political" with "non-legal." It is not surprising that the government of Cyprus emphasizes international law in its foreign policy. Grotius would approve.

Nor is it particularly surprising that the British government, vis-à-vis the Cyprus situation at least, has had a habit of shirking its responsibilities. The legalistic pirouetting on the question of Britain's Commonwealth obligations, if Cyprus were attacked, is a case in point: if Australia or New Zealand were threatened, Britain "would be immediately involved."[17] But no such luck for fellow Commonwealth member Cyprus: after extended correspondence in the sixties about Britain's obligations, which included various interpretations of the nuances of, and relations between, the words "obligation," "commitment," "moral," and "political," the imprecise phrase "general obligations arising from common membership of the Commonwealth" was agreed on.[18] The adjective "general" is notoriously flexible.

The lack of legal precision on the part of partition-mongers is confined not only to the supranational aspects of international law, but also to the very

treaties that established the republic. These treaties are imbued with a dangerous lack of clarity that has been exploited to the detriment of genuine peace
and stability. British policy formulation vis-à-vis the treaties has been incon-
sistent and even contradictory: at the height of the 1967 crisis, the FCO asked
the Law Officer's Department whether, under the Treaty of Guarantee, Britain
was obliged to take unilateral action to protect Cyprus from a possible Turkish
invasion. They replied that no such obligation was imposed by the treaty.

Use of the word "imposed" is significant, since there is an obvious im-
plication that such an obligation existed. Before looking more closely, let us
quote Article 4 of the treaty:

> In the event of a breach of the present treaty, Greece, Turkey and the United
> Kingdom undertake to consult together with respect to the representations or
> measures necessary to ensure observance of these provisions. In so far that
> common or concerted action may not prove possible, each of the three guar-
> anteeing powers reserves the right to take action with the sole aim of reestab-
> lishing the state of affairs created by the present treaty.

They justified their opinion that the treaty did not impose an obligation, by
saying that if Article 4 were breached, the three powers would only be obliged
to consult: if concerted action proved impossible, there was no obligation on
any of the three powers to take unilateral action, since the treaty merely reserved the right.

If we try to interpret this contorted and obtuse language, they were
claiming that reserving the right to act unilaterally did not mean that a guarantor power was automatically obliged to do so. This appears contradictory,
since it renders Article 4, and therefore the treaty, otiose and even
meaningless. Having thus muddied the waters, the law officers then "dealt
with" the arguments as to what Britain's obligations would be if Cyprus itself
were to invoke the treaty and ask Britain to protect it from an attack. They
claimed that Britain would be entitled to reject such a request because of
numerous breaches of the treaty by the Cypriot government. Here, they were
treading on thin legalistic ice. First, they were rendering the treaty null and
void; second, two wrongs do not make a right; and third, some of the alleged
breaches, such as appointing Greek Cypriots to ministerial posts reserved for
Turkish Cypriots, were necessary because of the latter's refusal to participate.
In addition, the constitution had become unworkable, as the British
government readily admitted.

Particularly significant in this obscure and intellectually sloppy argumentation, however, was the fact that they acknowledged the Cypriot government's view that the Treaty of Guarantee was contrary to Article 2.4 of the UN
Charter and completely overridden by Article 103, by saying that it was "not
without force." Indeed, this typical understatement really means that they
tended strongly toward the Cypriot government's view. They concluded by
stating that forcible intervention in Cyprus by the United Kingdom or Greece
at the request of the Cypriot government and to protect it against Turkish invasion would not be contrary to the charter.[19] This typically coy understatement
actually meant that such action would be in line with the charter.

The Foreign Office's reaction to the law officers' advice was both contradictory and dilatory: when a senior official wished to ask the law officers to clarify their advice, he was overruled by the chief legal adviser, on the spurious grounds that the law officers had been very reserved about intervention without the permission of the Cyprus government. Yet, they had made it quite clear that this would be unlawful and in breach of the UN Charter. The inability, or express tactic, of not seeking clarity on the issue was sinister, particularly in view of the decision not to intervene three years earlier, if Turkey were to invade (see chapter 2, page 29). It is hardly surprising that the Foreign Office advised the foreign secretary to avoid becoming involved in questions about the effects of the provisions of the Treaty of Guarantee and of Establishment, and the extent of Britain's obligations under them,[20] nor that the Foreign Office admitted that embassies could not be expected to handle successfully arguments on "the questions on Article 103 of the Charter and the Treaty of Guarantee."[21]

The whole question of the legality of the treaties establishing Cyprus was complicated by the fact that the FCO considered them to be a single package. The following quote shows how the whole package was closely connected to the SBAs:

> The abandonment of our position on the Treaty of Guarantee would undermine our position on the rest of the 1960 settlement . . . anything which called the 1960 settlement as a whole into question could expose us to pressure on our moral (as distinct from legal) right to hang on to the areas.[22]

It is, therefore, easy to understand, given this background, and looking at the admittedly tedious nitty-gritty of policy-formulation, how partition-friendly the whole treaty package was, and why the new state got off to such a shaky start. It was clear that the Treaty of Guarantee was a paper tiger which Britain was loath to honor. In this sense, it was the question of the British territories which undermined any chance of improving the constitution. It follows that the SBAs served as a poison for the whole treaty package. After all, even if the bases were separate legally from the republic, the fact that a huge part of the Treaty of Guarantee was devoted to those very bases made a mockery of legalistic attempts to separate the issues. Following the invasion, the FCO wrote in a policy paper:

> Following the decision not to use military force in Cyprus and the relatively small amount of pressure we can bring to bear on Cyprus, Greece and Turkey, this puts us in the invidious position of having responsibility without power. This has brought us no advantages whatsoever and it must be in British interests to work for a solution which will not involve Britain in any guarantee obligations or other lasting commitments over Cyprus. Such a solution is however remote and will be particularly difficult to achieve as long as we retain a physical presence in the Bases.[23]

The invasion that led to such comments highlights the double standards of the Turkish government in claiming any legality whatsoever in its occupation and in its negotiating methods. Despite its claim that it acted on the basis of the Treaty of Guarantee, it violated the 1960 accords themselves, as well as the NATO Charter.[24] The British government in particular, was, despite its public head-in-the-sand stance on the occupation, scathing in its private assessment of how the Turkish government treated the law:

> One implication of the current Turkish Cypriot constitutional moves, and specifically of Denktash's confirmation to me that they regard the post of President and Vice-President as having lapsed, is the extent to which the whole 1960 treaty apparatus be held to have lapsed . . . we . . . continue to regard the 1960 constitution as still in practice operative, despite the various derogations by both Greek and Turkish Cypriots since 1963. But the Turkish side is in effect saying increasingly openly and firmly that the 1960 constitution is defunct. They are of course freely having their cake and eating it by applying the view only when it suits them.[25]

> It is not, however, open to the Turkish Government to pick and choose between the various parts of the 1960 Treaty apparatus as it suits their purposes . . . the Turks cannot rely on the collapse of the Constitution in order to justify intervention for the purpose of re-establishing the state of affairs established by the basic Articles of the Constitution and, having intervened with that aim, then ignore that aim because the Constitution has lapsed.[26]

From the perspective of both the UN Charter and the treaties, it is evident that, apart from the complexity of the whole pastiche of confusing legalistic argument, Cyprus's constitution is burdened by the imprecision of the 1960 treaties and their connection with the SBAs, imprecision which has, if not caused, at least facilitated, the occupation and partition that still exists. We now take leave of the legal aspects of the Cyprus situation and turn to the emotive question of morality, which is clearly connected to the clash between law and immorality.

Morality and Reality: Difficult Bedfellows

Our weary world is well aware of the periodic spasms of blatant hypocrisy in the conduct of international relations, during which, all too often, expediency and selectivity are the order of the day. International politics, like national politics, can bring out the worst in human nature. Looking for morality in international relations is like looking for a needle in a haystack, just as are the desperate attempts by politicians to justify unilateral attacks on sovereign states, inevitably citing humanitarianism, morality, and ethics to obscure the basest of motives. But sometimes, the only ethics involved are business ethics, which is in any case often an oxymoronic term. Moralistic sloganizing by leading politicians of the ilk of Bush and Blair, such as "crusade" and "axis of evil," disguise extreme cynicism. Consider this statement, made as far back as 1998: "Among the nations of the world, only the United States has the moral standing, and the means to back it up . . . Our cause is just, our cause is moral, our cause is right."[27]   In the well-known scandal of the attack on Iraq, justified on a lie, the idea was to export "Western freedom." Instead, hundreds of thousands of innocent people were killed (and are still being killed at the time of writing), and the country destabilized, at least for the immediate future, with the possibility that it will end up split into different enclaves, like Afghanistan, creating ever more tension in the Middle East. As for the morality of "extraordinary renditions," a euphemism for "torture flights," the less said, the better.   In the case of Cyprus, there was a hope that George Bush Senior's pompously announced "New World Order" after the alleged end of the Cold War would have a beneficial knock-on effect, particularly following the reunification of Germany. This proved to be illusory, with Turkey continuing to consolidate its destructive division. Pseudo-morality in the interest of interests took precedence over balance and international law.

Although precise parallels can rarely be drawn between two events, some comparisons can be made between the Cyprus situation and other ones, if only to underline the double standards involved, and which show that at the end of the day, expediency and profits tend to take priority over peace and principles, whatever the indignant huffing and puffing of some politicians. We can juxtapose Britain's refusal to honor its obligations in Cyprus with its declaration of war on Germany in both world wars, on the grounds that Germany had violated Belgian neutrality and invaded Poland, respectively. In the first case, Britain honored its treaty obligations, while in the second, Britain also did, although it expediently ignored the fact that it should also have invaded the Soviet Union, since the latter also invaded Poland. When Iraq invaded Kuwait (itself artificially sliced off from Iraq by the British!), Britain was quick to join the United States in condemning Saddam Hussein and come to Kuwait's aid.[28]   The United States and Britain protected the Kurds of Iraq for strategic reasons but have treated those of Turkey as terrorists, when there is very little to choose between the two groups. No such luck for the 200,000 Cypriots forced out of their homes and expelled southwards, despite Britain's legal commitments. In fact, quite the opposite was the case, even for British subjects in Cyprus being harassed by the Turkish army, but British subjects with Greek names. The Foreign Office wrote: "It may therefore be necessary at some stage to take the decision that their interests must be put at risk or even sacrificed."[29]   The British subjects in the Malvinas/Falkland Islands were of British stock, and were rescued, in stark contrast to those of Diego Garcia (who had brown skins) and who were expelled from their homelands to Mauritius with minimum compensation to accommodate the wishes of its new military tenants, the United States. There is a parallel here to be drawn with Cyprus, in that Britain carved off territory from both Cyprus and Mauritius during the independence process. In the case of Cyprus, *de facto* annexation was the method, while in the case of Mauritius, Britain acquired the Chagos Islands, renaming them the British Indian Ocean Territories, so that at independence Britain had its strategic foothold in the area, just as in Cyprus. Perhaps if Cyprus had had a group of suitable islands, Britain would have carved them off instead, but this is, of course, a hypothetical moot point. In the case of Diego Garcia, the British gassed all the islanders' pets and livestock before expelling the islanders to Mauritius.[30] In this respect, at least, the Cypriots were luckier.

We can see, then, that we need a bucket of salt when discussing the morals of the Cyprus situation. The situation is by definition eminently immoral, and we therefore now need to spell out the actions undertaken by Turkey in the attempt to artificially cement the division and occupation. First is the obvious immorality of not only the mass expulsions of Greek Cypriots, but also of their replacement with illegal Anatolian settlers, to the extent that the ratio of settlers to Turkish Cypriots (we shall consider this in the following chapter) is now 2:1, a ratio that does not include the occupying soldiers.[31] We can see that a key characteristic of the Turkish invasion and division involves manipulating the demographic structure of the Muslim Turkish-speaking people of Cyprus themselves, and not only bludgeoning through the massive displacement of their Greek-speaking homologues.

Since crime surely comes under the immorality rubric, we need to mention usurpation of property. The most recent evidence of the immorality of Turkish actions was the European Court of Justice's judgment in favor of the owner of a property in occupied Cyprus, Meletios Apostolides, against a British couple, David and Linda Orams, who had somehow "bought" his land. They have been ordered to return the land to its rightful owner, pay compensation, and demolish the house they built on the land. Significantly, the Oramses lost their appeal on 19 January 2010, with the court referring to the United Kingdom's international obligations, in particular the obligation to respect the independence, territorial integrity, and security of the Republic of Cyprus, as set out in the Treaty of Guarantee. This case again emphasizes the unworkability of the current Turkish proposals for Cyprus. It would not be politic to comment on them in detail at this stage, however, since discussions are continuing as this book is going into print. There are over five thousand British nationals living on stolen property in occupied Cyprus.[32] This landmark case will naturally lead to thousands of Cypriots being awarded compensation, as well as having their ownership confirmed. Perhaps one of the most distasteful aspects of the case was that Cherie Blair, the wife of the then British prime minister, represented the Orams in a case that had clear political and moral undertones that went far beyond the strictly legal. The result shows that a viable and functional federation will only be achieved with the central involvement of the EU, rather than through Annan-type derogations that both undermine the EU itself and create tension and further unnatural and illegal partition. Another well-known case, but by no means the only one, is that of Titina Loizidou, who eventually won her case at the European Court of Human Rights and was paid compensation, although the Turkish government still refused to let her have her property. The reason that Turkey could no longer go on flouting the court willy-nilly, as it had with various judgments, was the pressure applied by the Council of Europe's Committee of Ministers, which declared its intention to ensure by all means available Turkey's compliance. Worried about the status of its EU application, Turkey had to pay. The Loizidou case is, of course, but one of a whole huge backlog of cases, an embarrassment to Turkey's supporters, who saw the Annan Plan (see above, page 40) as an expedient way of solving the problem. Perhaps the most significant aspect of the case was that Turkey had tried to avoid it by claiming that it was the responsibility of the illegal "TRNC," a claim the court rejected. It shows that Turkey has in fact simply annexed the northern part of Cyprus, whatever claims it may make about it being an independent state. Another, but no less important aspect, is that the government of Cyprus is considered responsible for the whole island, and that the occupying power is, therefore, *in flagrante delicto.*

Property apart, people themselves have been violated. In this connection, in 1976 the European Commission of Human Rights (ECHR) found that Turkey was responsible for inhumane treatment in the wake of the invision. Turkey was found to have violated various articles of the European Convention, including those on right to life, liberty, and security of the person, and respect or private and family life. The *Sunday Times* described the judgment as "a horrendous indictment against Turkey."[33] In 1983, the commission passed a similar judgment. We do not have the space to list the numerous judgments against Turkey, other than to mention a recent ruling (embarrassingly late) by the ECHR against Turkey in a case brought against it by the relatives of missing Greek Cypriots, stating that it had failed to conduct an effective investigation into their whereabouts and fate. It goes without saying that such barbaric acts contravene the Fourth Geneva Convention. Needless to say, they had the desired effect and encouraged the Greek Cypriots to flee. In an intriguing contrast, in January 1975, 2,577 of the 11,967 Turkish Cypriots who had fled into the British base at Akrotiri returned to their homes in the free part of Cyprus.[34] It is perhaps telling that Callaghan, clearly smarting from his experience at the Geneva conferences, during which he received reports of Turkish "activities," told Kissinger: "Now as regards Greece and Turkey, it is Greece who will need massaging because the Turks are too jingoistic, indeed too close to Hitler for my liking."[35] To help us to gain some insight into the nature of the jingoism mentioned above by Callaghan, and how it has obscured and twisted morality, a "Hymn of Hate" makes for some unfortunate reading. It could make even the most extreme Greek Cypriot blush.

As long as vengeance fills my veins
As long as my heart beats for Turkism
As long as the word "Greek" exists in dictionaries
By Allah, this hate will not leave me
A thousand heads of the Greeks will not wash away this hate.

I will crush the heads of 10,000 of them
I will throw into the sea the bodies of 30,000 of them
But by Allah this hate will never leave me
A thousand heads of the Greeks will not wash away this hate.

As long as my fists can stand up in the air
As long as 120,000 hearts can beat together
As long as 40 million [Turks] support me
By Allah this hate will not leave me
A thousand heads of the Greeks will not wash away this hate.[36]

This was recited on the first anniversary of the invasion. It suggests a certain amount of propagandistic interference from extreme Turkish organizations such as the "Grey Wolves," since the Turkish Cypriots are a peaceful people who lived calmly with their Greek-speaking neighbors for centuries, until Britain cynically but mistakenly brought Turkey into the equation. It has to be said that although there were some atrocities committed by Greek Cypriot irregulars, particularly in 1963/4, which understandably embittered some Turkish Cypriots, there were far more Turkish ones, particularly in 1958, when Turkish-sponsored TMT extremists attacked the Greek Cypriots, and, of course, in 1974. But many wrongs do not make a right. Since the invasion, all the wrongs have been committed by Turkey, which was recently found guilty by the ECHR of human rights violations in the brutal killings of Anastasios Isaak and Solomos Solomou in 1996. During demonstrations in the buffer zone, Solomou was shot dead by a Turkish Grey Wolf fanatic as he tried to scale the Turkish flagpole, while Isaak was beaten to death by fanatics of a similar ilk. Thankfully, the climate has undergone a major change since then, as we shall see in our concluding chapter. The fanatics are beginning to crawl back under their stones.

Before moving on to the economic aspects of the forced division of the island, we need to mention the systematic destruction of a cultural heritage that goes back some eleven thousand years. At the time of writing, cemeteries in some twenty-five villages have been desecrated and destroyed, 229 churches have been completely desecrated, 100 churches have been turned into mosques, 67 turned into farm buildings, 57 have become museums, cultural centers, or hotels, and 25 have been demolished, a total of 520.[37] Archaeological sites and monasteries have been damaged and systematically looted, with various artifacts and treasures finding their way into foreign auction rooms, some being returned following vigorous legal action.[38] Generally speaking, and to end our look at the moral aspects of partition, we can say that the ethnic cleansing, the changing of place names, the systematic importing of non-Cypriots, and the destroying of the Christian, Hellenic, and European aspects of occupied Cyprus has constituted a planned attempt to impose the customs and traditions of a foreign country on its annexed territory. The economic factors in this turkification process are no less needful of mention.

Schizophrenic Economy

Despite dire predictions of economic problems in the free part of Cyprus in the wake of the invasion, owing to the massive influx of refugees and the occupation of the most productive parts of the island, it was in the medium term the Turkish Cypriots who suffered, notwithstanding the damage done to the Greek Cypriots' lives and properties in the northern part of the island. Even with factories and houses expropriated from the Greek Cypriots and the incipient influx of illegal settlers, the situation in occupied Cyprus was woesome, as the following extract from a British high commissioner's annual review shows:

> The disproportion between the two communities is nowhere more evident than in their relative economic progress during the past year . . . The Greek Cypriots have faced the challenge with their traditional vigour and commercial acumen. . . . Meanwhile the picture on the Turkish side is one of almost unrelieved gloom. Statistics are hard to come by, and when produced are difficult to credit. But observation and discussion reveal that only a few of the newly-acquired factories have been brought into effective operation, that agricultural production particularly in the citrus sector has fallen short of its potential, that prices are generally high and shortages evident. The Turkish Cypriots suffer from a critical lack at all levels of administrative, technical, skilled and semi-skilled manpower . . . the heavy subsidies from Turkey will continue.[39]

We shall not now dwell on economic history, but rather demonstrate that the unnatural and aggressive partition has proven to be illogical economically and detrimental to the interests of the Turkish Cypriots. The main point is that a large discrepancy has developed between the two communities as a result of the partition, to the extent that the partition is economically warped. Figures can sometimes speak louder than words: in 1960, GDP *per capita* in the area now occupied by the Turkish army was 86 percent of the Cypriot average, but had fallen to 65 percent by 1977, some three years after the invasion. Despite the subsequent allegedly free development of an allegedly independent "state," GDP in the north had fallen to only 33 percent by 1993.[40] This was due largely to the weak Turkish lira, which the north had no choice but to adopt, and to the inefficiency and corruption of public administrative structures. The situation has alleviated somewhat, but only because the economy of the north is essentially integrated with that of Turkey and receives handouts. More importantly, not being recognized as a state by any country but Turkey (a curiosity, since it is essentially annexed territory rather than an independent state), foreign criminals, especially those on the run, live and invest in Cyprus, owing to the difficulty of their being extradited: on the one hand, the legal government is responsible for extradition questions but can do nothing, while on the other, the Turkish government has claimed that the "government" of the "TRNC" is responsible. The only way, therefore, of extraditing a criminal from occupied Cyprus is to recognize the occupation regime, which, of course, no member of the UN can do, since this would be tantamount to recognizing international crime. Having a grey/black economy has its benefits, but mainly for those who prefer to break the law, rather than for the native Turkish Cypriots.[41] Perhaps the most notorious was Asil Nadir, who absconded from Britain to occupied Cyprus under controversial circumstances while awaiting trial on theft and fraud charges.

The year 2003 is significant, as it marks the easing of crossing restrictions along the UN ceasefire line which had been imposed by the Turkish occupation forces since 1974. Other measures began to benefit occupied Cyprus. Turkish Cypriots can now work in free Cyprus, and several thousand do, although precise statistics are tricky, owing to current market volatility. They receive medical and social insurance and, along with Turkish Cypriots visiting from occupied Cyprus, free medical treatment. This is, of course, possible, because virtually all the Turkish Cypriots have applied for, and been granted, Republic of Cyprus passports, identity cards, or birth certificates. This has relieved to a certain extent the burden imposed by the illegal settlers and by living under an occupation regime. Many Turkish Cypriot children also receive free private schooling. On top of this, the republic has supplied a large amount of free water and electricity to Turkish Cypriots. Nevertheless, the economy of the north is itself illegitimate, hence its reputation as a haven for international criminals. There is also some fast money to be made by supplying cheap degrees through quickly established over-the-counter colleges which have no real academic standards, but which nevertheless spray on a thin veneer of pseudo-academic respectability, even if the colleges, some styling themselves as "universities," are not recognized by serious institutions. They are a good earner of foreign currency, since fees usually have to be paid in euros or American dollars, and youngsters desperate to buy a degree are attracted. Construction on usurped Greek Cypriot properties is also a particularly lucrative business, as the above-mentioned case of the Orams demonstrates (page 67). The result has nevertheless been a slow improvement in the occupied areas, the *per capita* GNP of which was in 2004 about half that of the free areas of the republic, which is at $23,000.[42] If we add to this the millions of euros spent by visiting Greek Cypriots, then it is not difficult to begin to see that reunification is not simply a moral imperative but a crying socio-economic need, logical into the bargain. The absurdity of the continuing occupation increases almost by the hour and is indeed beginning to assume almost surrealistic proportions: on the one hand, we have a particularly democratic EU member striving to reunite the island on strictly European norms and, therefore, on a basis of equality, while on the other, a shrinking original Turkish Cypriot population is being swamped by a linguistically related, but nevertheless culturally and historically alien one. Politically, the situation can also be seen as somewhat absurd, but also dangerous. Economically, the Turkish Cypriot community would benefit enormously in terms of convergence, if there were a genuine functional re-unification. At the present, however, economic volatility stems from money laundering, illegal casinos, drug trafficking, and other criminal activity.

Political Dangers

In Cyprus, the nature of partition is such that the dangers are usually sensed when a stalemate is approaching and felt when the stalemate begins to become malignant. This was arguably the case in the late fifties, early sixties, and early seventies, when extremist groups from Greece and Turkey combined with certain angry politicians and officials, with President Makarios deftly dancing in their midst, no mean task. We have seen the results and need not dwell on them, but shall look at ways of finding a solution in our concluding chapter. The Cyprus situation is actually more immediately dangerous at the regional and international levels, in terms of what we shall call the "me-too" factor. There are plenty of secessionist organizations in Europe and elsewhere who are looking closely at the Cyprus situation, since the more that illegal

Cyprus is acknowledged, the harder they will push for secession. It was not surprising that Turkey immediately recognized Kosovo on its unilateral declaration of independence, which has already hardened the *de facto* sub-partition of the province: if Kosovo were ever to be fully recognized and become a UN member (unlikely in its present form), then Turkey would, of course, push even harder for recognition for its illegally occupied territory. The fact that the situations hardly bear historical comparison, given that Turkey took part of a sovereign state by force, while Albania did not invade Kosovo, which was, rather, entered by NATO following the reluctant withdrawal of the legal army, does not seem to concern the "me-too" people, who are often simple opportunists latching onto the "humanitarian" argument, even if there are no lives to be saved.

The main danger, however, lies within the EU. This is because the rushed expansion following Germany's reunification threw a wrench in the organizational and ideological works, thus helping centrifugal forces to negatively exploit the historical trend toward ever closer union, a trend necessary to keep the nationalists at bay and make even the very idea of war, in Europe at least, a primitive and outdated concept. The new East European members, particularly Poland, the Czech Republic, and Hungary, are certainly a long way psychologically from feeling at home with the original concept of the Six, based on a Franco-German model. They are more interested in their relations with the United States, to enable them to atavistically face down what they see as neo-Stalinism to their east and balance the United States against the Germans to their west. While the somewhat non-*communautaire* attitude of such members continues, this does not help the Cyprus situation, which depends to an important extent on European "centripetalism." It is, however, "centrifugalism" which has recently been making itself felt. It was demonstrated most graphically when the centrifugal East Europeans supported the Anglo-Americans, while the EU backbone, France and Germany, came out against the attack on Iraq. We witnessed a similar phenomenon in 2009, when the governments of the Czech Republic and Poland tried to station U.S. anti-missile radar shields on their territories, to the considerable irritation of Russia and the consternation of France and Germany. In such a climate, it is in Cyprus's interests to be traditionally *communautaire*, since the more centripetal, and therefore integrationist, EU members become, the more difficult it becomes for anti-integrationist, and often secessionist, forces, which are intent on breaking up the union as a serious political and military entity. The interesting aspect of Cyprus's membership is that the republic joined as a split land but is now doing its best to bring matters back to normal. It is perhaps a sign of the EU's subtle power that it was able to stomach the membership of a partially occupied country, with the occupied bit having displayed externally provoked secessionist tendencies. Cyprus's EU accession was expected to lead to a natural reunification, under the *acquis communautaire*, and an end to the occupation, but Turkey has thus far proved incapable of displaying the European behavior necessary to bring this about.

The danger of the occupation is that the longer Turkey persists with its occupation and cultural desertification policy, the worse it becomes for the Turkish Cypriots, who now have less control over their own affairs than ever, having been swamped by Turkish soldiers and settlers (see next chapter). It is also dangerous for European integration, since Turkish policy vis-à-vis Cyprus and the Aegean are a major obstacle in establishing a common European defense policy and serious, functional future European armed forces. We shall devote some space to this in our concluding chapter. In this sense, the Turkish occupation is holding the smooth-running of the European project to ransom. To sum up on the political aspects of the Cyprus situation, it is clear that it reinforces two threats to European stability. One is the "me-too" syndrome, while the other, clearly connected, is "centrifugalism" *per se*. We now turn to the practical problems engendered by aggressive partition.

Practical Questions

The situation in the Turkish-occupied north is indeed unique, not to say bizarre, in terms of the practicalities of everyday living and the status of the population internationally. Most interesting is that the Turkish Cypriots have continued to accept the opportunity offered by the legal government for obtaining Republic of Cyprus passports, identity cards, and birth certificates which they are entitled to as citizens of the Republic of Cyprus. Thus, the bizarre situation exists in which Turkish Cypriots living in the occupied areas nevertheless recognize the Republic of Cyprus. They have EU benefits and the security of being in charge of their own lives, even though they are living in occupied and unrecognized territory. Yet, in relation to Turkey, they can be seen as second-class citizens, since they are living in land invaded and taken by force from their internationally recognized government, and have themselves been swamped by the Anatolian settlers, sent and encouraged to settle by a government that claims to recognize them as independent (see next chapter).

Conversely, the settlers, though favored (by Turkey) citizens vis-à-vis the native inhabitants, nevertheless have a high risk of not owning their own lives. After all, living in someone else's home cannot be a particularly solid experience, with the sword of Damocles waiting to reestablish justice for those expelled. Moreover, as "Cypriots," they are internationally unrecognized and are in this respect, therefore, second-class citizens in relation to the Turkish Cypriots and even non-citizens internationally. They are primarily Turks, and only substitute Cypriots, and cannot, obviously, enjoy the benefits of the Turkish Cypriots themselves, who are citizens of the Republic of Cyprus.

Conclusions

The cynical manipulation by Turkey of the messy constitutional arrangements imposed on Cyprus in 1960 is a major factor in Cyprus's current situation. Without Turkey's partitionist and predatory designs, things might well have turned out for the better. Comparing the island to another area where the British were responsible, Palestine, we see that the island is at least primarily Cypriot, something that no one has ever disputed, whereas the territory of Palestine has transmogrified into Palestinians, Israelis, Israeli Arabs (so labeled by the Israelis), West Bankers, Jerusalemites, Gazans, and Jordanians. Nomenclature becomes a sport, as when some Arab delegations walk out at UN conferences where the Israelis present papers on "Judea" and "Samaria."[43] The name "Cyprus" is at least onomastically indisputable and shows little danger of division into more than its two free and occupied Cypriot and two British parts (the FCO has in the past referred to the bases as being as British as Cornwall, although, unlike in Cornwall, there are no members of Parliament!). We have seen how legally precarious the idea of partition is generally, and how illegal in the specific case of Cyprus; how immoral it has turned out to be, in terms of international law, but also regarding basic human decency; how impractical and unworkable the divided economy has turned out to be, with only free Cyprus functioning normally economically, while the economy of occupied Cyprus is neither viable nor self-supporting; how dangerous an example "partitionism" can be for political opportunists throughout Europe and indeed elsewhere, and how dangerous for EU cohesion *per se*; and how thoroughly impractical the whole arrangement is. We devote our next chapter to a closer look at these inhabitants and their regime in occupied Cyprus, and how partition has affected what was once a peaceful and beautiful area.

CHAPTER SIX

Indigenous Population versus Uninvited Guests

Never in the field of human conflict was so much owed by so many to so few.[1]

Introduction

Turkey has pursued a systematic policy of colonization since taking a large slice of Cyprus. It has so far not only replaced almost all the expelled Greek Cypriots but also swamped the indigenous Turkish Cypriots, many of whom have emigrated in despair, to London and Australia in particular. The status of the inhabitants of occupied Cyprus is understandably vague and imprecise, and would have been even more so under the Annan Plan. We have already seen how selfish foreign interests, interference, legal imprecision, semantic chicanery, and sheer intellectual laziness can be characteristics of a partitionist mentality. We shall attempt here to clarify what it means to live in occupied territory and show how the original inhabitants are increasingly becoming spectators, in their own land, of a crude but systematic geopolitical ethnic manipulation on a par with the expulsion of Greek-speaking Christians of the Ottoman Empire in 1923, the ejection of Germans by Poland, and the replacement of expelled Palestinians in the late forties and thereafter.

Turkish Control

Lest there be any lingering doubt about the administration of occupied Cyprus as being under the firm control of Ankara, with only cosmetic lipstick service being applied to local decision-making, the European Court of Human Rights, in its judgment in the above-mentioned Loizidou case (page 67), stated that Turkey had effective overall control over the "TRNC," which was a "subordinate local administration." Let us look at this a little more closely in order to better understand the nature of Ankara's aim of partition. First is the fact that the leadership of the Turkish Cypriot community has been under the effective control of the Turkish military since 1 August 1958, when command of the Turkish Defense Force (TMT) was given to a Turkish mainland officer.[2] This became even more pronounced during and following the 1963/64 troubles. Unlike the Turkish Cypriots, the Greek Cypriots had Makarios, head of a legitimate government, to counterbalance extremist influence from Athens. Turkish *de facto* control increased as the stalemate continued: by 1972, the British high commissioner was writing that the Turkish Cypriot administration was beholden to the Turkish government.[3] There is, of course, more to it than that, since "Turkish government" is not specific enough a term to reveal the full extent of the "deep state," a kind of military-industrial complex with secularist leanings and difficult to define precisely, although it is in essence the hard core of the armed forces. The following extract from a British high commissioner's report elaborates and clarifies matters to some extent:

> Despite all this Governmental activity the Administration is far from being a government in the full sense of the word, since it is beholden in different ways to two authorities outside its own control. The first of these is the Turkish Government. Apart from strong ties of every kind with the Motherland, and the Pro-Consular position of the Turkish Embassy here, this relationship has a more mysterious side. In the Administration's laws, operational control of the armed forces, the police, the civil defence forces etc., is attributed to a shadowy individual with a variety of code names and cover names—the Standard Bearer (Bayraktar), the Grey Wolf (Bozkurt) or even the Competent Authority (Ilgili Makam). This individual is not appointed by the Administration but is a serving Turkish officer introduced into Cyprus by the Turkish General Staff under diplomatic cover. His existence is never officially admitted by the Turkish Embassy or by the Turkish Cypriots. It is for this reason that both we and the UN peacekeeping force find negotiations with the Turkish Cypriots so frustrating . . . In all military and security matters the Bozkurt's word is law. How his responsibilities are defined and how far his power extends are obscure, both to us and to the Turkish Cypriots themselves.[4]

It would be naive to think, at the very least, that the shadowy grey wolf is not still in control where it matters to the Turkish armed forces. A Turkish Cypriot expert states that the north is governed by the "National Coordinating Council," exercising supreme power over the legislative, executive, and judicial branches of the "TRNC." It consists of the Turkish ambassador, the (Turkish) commander of the occupation forces, the (Turkish) commander of the security forces, and the president, prime minister, and deputy prime minister of the "TRNC."[5] The police are also under the direct control of the Turkish army.[6] In a blatant piece of psychological arm-twisting, a Turkish commander told conscripts at the end of 2003 that Turkish Cypriots who support a solution to the Cyprus problem were enemy collaborators.[7] As one expert has made clear, the TMT was decided at the highest level in Ankara and run from there.[8] Although both the National Front for the Liberation of Cyprus (EMAK) and EOKA, its successor, made it clear that they considered the Turkish Cypriots as friends and allies, the TMT called on Turkish Cypriot youths to oppose EOKA.[9] Although it no longer officially exists, its malign and extremist influence does, sometimes in the form of the Grey Wolves. Just as throughout 1957 the TMT told the Turkish Cypriots to disengage from the Greek

Cypriots, so a Turkish Cypriot journalist (see below) was harassed and falsely imprisoned at Ankara's instigation.

Before looking at the implications of the above for the genuine Turkish Cypriots, a final quote by a senior Turkish politician serves us well:

> Today the TRNC is only a republic on paper. The money, everything goes there from Turkey. Even the Turkish ambassador cannot do anything without the permission of the military commander there. All the large investments in Northern Cyprus are given to tenders . . . , directly in Ankara. This means that Northern Cyprus is governed like a province of Turkey.[10]

Such a situation is obviously an irritant to any, even only vaguely minded, believer in democracy. Let us consider one well-known case.

From Europe to Africa

This heading seems a *non sequitur*. But it epitomizes the absurdity of the occupation and the enormous democratic deficit in the illegal "TRNC," which is no fault of the moderate Turkish Cypriots, who are still bravely trying to eke out a reasonable existence, despite the problems of being occupied. *Avrupa* (Europe) was a Turkish Cypriot newspaper edited by Shener Levent which, because of its democratic views, was attacked. Levent was arrested and held incommunicado for a while without charge and questioned by a Turkish general. Following a trial on trumped-up charges of spying, he was acquitted (but not before "doing time" without charge), thanks largely to the international publicity given to his case by Greek Cypriot friends. So, in a *tour d'adresse* of considerable acumen, he changed the name of the newspaper to *Afrika*. To shed light on his apparent crime, a quote from his book will serve, as it encapsulates his previously published views, albeit with considerable feeling, and epitomizes the plight of the Turkish Cypriots:

> After going through so much pain, we should have become more humane, isn't that the case? But no, every time the sad anniversary of 1974 comes up, we gather over the graves of those killed, holding crosses or crescents, depending on our faith and still preaching words that smell of blood . . . Instead of apologising a thousand times over to our beloved dead, instead of carrying our crimes on our backs to our own Golgotha, we swear to commit the same crimes once again . . . Really, though, this is not the kind of people we are . . . Our chests bear the fragrance of jasmine and do not reek of hatred, rancour and revenge. We ache in our desire to unite our love in Greek and Turkish, on a cool veranda, in summer days. As neighbours, we warned each other of danger and saved each other, even at times of bitter conflict. . . . We cannot accept a divided homeland. Neither Paphos nor the Karpass Peninsula can be kept behind borders. It is others who filled our lives with such habits and set up ambushes in our own land . . . This homeland is our own! It belongs to us,

my friends! All of us! All Cypriots! We want neither unification with mother countries nor division! Until the last foreign soldier leaves our land![11]

It is easy to see why this sort of viewpoint, particularly from a Turkish Cypriot, is anathema to the partitionist Turkish state, at least the bit of it that conceals the Bozkurt. It is perhaps curious that whenever there has been the possibility of serious talks between the two communities, without outside interference, they have been scotched by extreme forces, such as in 1963, when the Thirteen Points should have been discussed rather than provoke an extreme Turkish reaction, which in turn fired up the Greek Cypriots. And in 1974, when progress was being made, it was then frustrated by clumsy and pernicious extremist external forces, mainly, but not exclusively, Greek, which gave the Turkish military the illicit window it was seeking to partition the island, and worse, to take the whole of Cyprus, something which would have led to all-out war between Greece and Turkey.

Demographic Dustbin[12]

The vast majority of settlers are from Turkey. Although completely precise and up-to-date numbers of settlers are hard to come by, it can be safely assumed that, given Turkey's high rate of unemployment, few would wish to return. Many complaints about the settlers from the diminishing core of original Turkish Cypriots have focused on the general question of changing the demographic structure, while others have been made in connection with the electoral register. What are the possible scenarios? First, we can envisage more Turkish Cypriots leaving, probably for London and Australia, while even more Anatolians pour in. The latest published information from the Cypriot government suggests that there are 160,000 illegal settlers, as against 59,000 Turkish Cypriots.[13] Naturally, a hard core could well remain, indeed, the very old would be unlikely to feel the urge to leave, unless it were to join their children. Many could, of course, return to their properties in free Cyprus, as some are beginning to. At any rate, in this scenario, we would see the eventual subsuming of the native Turkish Cypriots into the new and artificial demographic situation, with some "escaping," or returning to free areas, simply to preserve their identity. Another scenario is an increase in tension between the locals and the colonists which could manifest itself in open strife, if the younger, more lucrative-minded and adventurous section of the colonists take over what social services there are, and the more established locals begin to feel like strangers in their own land, confronted with settlers, most of whom have Turkish nationality. According to one expert, the settlers want only one third of the pay of the Turkish Cypriots, thus robbing them of a livelihood. It is hardly surprising that so many have already emigrated. The two groups even have their own cafes.[14] The most bizarre scenario would see most of the remaining Turkish Cypriots residing in the free areas of the republic and polishing their rusty Greek, with the occupied north remaining a *de facto* Anatolian province. Forcing people together, as Turkey has done in its occupied zone, can lead to tension, since it detracts from the "live and let live" principle of granting one's neighbor the space to breathe. This latter scenario, like the other two, is a threat to the future, essentially because Turkey's motive is military rather than social, and the absurdity of the occupation will become increasingly visible. It is significant that already twenty years ago, some two thousand retired Turkish officers and their dependents were living near the sea in former Greek Cypriot-owned villas, with another three thousand other ranks and their dependents living in slightly less luxurious houses. This was their reward for having "served" in Cyprus.[15]

The Myth of Isolation

Following the discarding of the Annan Plan, the Turkish government began a propaganda campaign, claiming that the Cypriot government was responsible for the Turkish Cypriots being isolated and at an economic disadvantage. This was the art of meta-myth at its most extreme. It is, after all, the Turkish government and armed forces which have kept the island's economy, institutions, and people divided, and which have created a lawless situation in occupied Cyprus. It has demonstrated as spurious its claim that it intervened to preserve the sovereignty and territorial integrity of Cyprus, by doing the precise opposite, and creating a dependent piece of territory. Now that some crossings are open, Turkish Cypriots, citizens of the Republic of Cyprus, can circulate freely, and, as we have seen, many actually work in free Cyprus. With regard to passports and identity cards, it was the Turkish government that prevented Turkish Cypriots from acquiring legal documents issued by the Republic of Cyprus until recently, when, embarrassed by negative publicity and wishing to create the impression of negotiating in good faith on the Annan scheme, and because of its EU application, Turkey relented. The alleged isolation of the Turkish Cypriots has in any case been created by Turkey itself. The Cypriot government itself has done its best to combat the situation, not only through the freedom of movement granted to Turkish Cypriots but also through the provision of essential services such as pensions and social security benefits, and free medical care and electricity, often in the face of Turkish opposition. What economic deprivation there has been in the north is a simple result of the low-paid illegal settlers (there in contravention of the 1949 Geneva Convention) who divert employment from the native Turkish Cypriots. Additionally, the introduction of the Turkish lira has had a somewhat isolationist effect financially. Again, this was inflicted by a foreign country and has nothing to do with the legal government of the republic. In short, any restrictions on the Turkish Cypriots are due to Turkey. As it is, the republic does its best for them, which is why they use Republic of Cyprus papers. Turkey is simply dividing the people of Cyprus and exploiting the isolation myth as a ploy to gain entry into the EU on its own terms. It comes across as a cynical application of the discredited power politics of a bygone era. Such behavior is, however, rebounding in a more general way, which of course has implications for Turkey's illegal grip on Cyprus: the French foreign minister recently expressed his shock at Turkish pressure over the appointment of the Danish prime minister as the next NATO secretary general. This in turn prompted one expert to write that Turkey wanted all the privileges of NATO and EU membership, while wishing to continue to occupy and divide Cyprus.[16] It is difficult to avoid the impression that Turkey wants to have its cake and eat it too, hence the absurdity of its keeping the Turkish Cypriots from enjoying full EU rights and benefits and then claiming that they are isolated. It is hoisting itself with its own petard. Claire Palley's seminal work sums up the real situation neatly:

> All Cypriots have been victims of the Republic of Turkey, and the responsibility for nearly all economic, emotional and physical "suffering" in Cyprus—other than the hardships of everyday life—lies with Turkey, as does "the plight" of Turkish Cypriots . . . much of their economic deprivation is due to the fact that that they have been economically squeezed out of their own labour market by low-paid Turkish migrants.[17]

Conclusions

We have seen in this brief look at the Turkish Cypriots, how detrimental Turkey's policy has been for them. The north is in fact not only occupied territory, but a veritable police "state." Since 2003, however, it has to be said that there has been a relaxing of overt Turkish control, although how much of this is genuine and how much due to public relations and the importance of paying lip service to the EU is still difficult to tell, particularly since Turkey is notoriously unstable politically and since the armed forces wield an inordinate amount of power, this being written into the constitution. The above-mentioned public murder of two Greek Cypriots by the Grey Wolves on the Green Line in 1996 (page 69) still lurks in the minds of civilized Cypriots, whether Greek- or Turkish-speaking. If the settlers continue to become established, this could lead, indeed already is leading, to the uprooting, mutilation, and possible annihilation of the Turkish Cypriot character, rather akin to a vicious sting in the tail for the descendants of the original settlers. Today, the native Turkish Cypriots are simply the damage resulting from Turkey's aggression, occupation, ethnic cleansing, and manipulation. *Plus ça change.*

CHAPTER SEVEN

The European Island

Failing to prepare is preparing to fail.[1]

Introduction

Cyprus serves as a fascinating case study and gauge of the state of relations between states. It demonstrates that, despite the high-flown theory and humanitarian doublespeak with which we are confronted almost daily, the state of these relations is in some respects really rather basic, and even primitive. The vital factors of human behavior and characteristics tend to be avoided in most proffered "solutions" to Cyprus's problems, which is perhaps why they are of limited value. People tend to avoid getting to the bone, let alone the marrow of issues, because they like theoretical and clean models, paradigms and formulae, backed up by politically correct sloganized language. They are frightened of basic truths, and thus rationalize themselves into serious negotiators, politicians, academics, and journalists, all earnestly trying to solve the problem while forgetting the role of greed, ambition and, above all, pride and insecurity, which are the root causes of the problem. They escape from reality, looking for the easy way out. Often, they are embarrassed by the fact that the problem is one of aggression and occupation, thinking that using the jargon of international relations will somehow sweeten the pill and detract from the obvious international crime that has been perpetrated. Terms like "window of opportunity" (opportunity), "state actor" (country), "intervention" (invasion), "extraordinary rendition" (kidnapping and torture) and, in the case of Cyprus, "seasonal workers" (illegal settlers/colonists) confuse the essential issues and detract from the nub of the problem. While they may sterilize the more unpleasant aspects, they take people away from the basic causes.

As long as the human factor is studiously avoided in the circus situation of an EU member being forcibly divided and mistreated by a predatory alien power and bickered over by various conflicting powers, in a crude geopolitical merry-go-round, the tougher it will be to find a just solution, and the more surrealistic the whole question will become, made even more so by the fact that the occupier is an applicant to join the club whose member it is occupying. The increasing tortoise-like solidity of the EU does, however, permit us to adopt a cautiously sanguine stance. This is because the association of

Cyprus with the institutional continuity of the EU can be used to positive effect, by allowing us to emphasize the absurdity of Cyprus's situation in an organization as reasonably civilized as the EU. The longer the anomaly of an EU member being occupied by an alien power continues, the more this will emphasize the legal dichotomy of the state of Cyprus's position, and how a European solution will become increasingly likely, simply by default. Matters are, however, complicated by the number of non-Cypriot stakeholders, like rats on Cyprus's back, and by the agreements reached to date. In this penultimate chapter, we shall consider the constraints on an ideal legal solution in conformity with international law and the idea of a bizonal, bicommunal federation, which has become the generally accepted catchphrase for a solution, although, as we shall see, it is open to interpretation. Then we shall consider the international context and the strengths, weaknesses, opportunities, and threats for Cyprus, its region, and the EU.

Federation

> You can't get two heads into one hat.[2]

In January 1977, as we have seen (page 35), President Makarios bravely bit the bullet, in a major historical compromise in the interests of peace, by agreeing with Turkish Cypriot leader Rauf Denktash on a solution that would grant the Turkish Cypriots a considerable degree of autonomy in the form of an independent, non-aligned bicommunal federal republic. Since then, it has to be said, Turkey, rather than reciprocate when given an inch, has, as we have seen, tried to take a mile, and exploited every available opportunity to solidify the partition of the island in a way that suggests, at best, an extreme form of confederation and, at worst, a forcibly colonized slave-state. Again, in the way of our friend Guicciardini, it is history that illuminates the present. For despite President Makarios's compromise, Turkey did not wish to endanger its partitionist efforts, as a result of which the Vienna intercommunal talks failed in April of the same year. As the British high commissioner in Cyprus put it in September 1977, it was particularly the Turkish side which was holding up progress, while Denktash did not want a settlement.[3]

In September 2008, President Christofias (see chapter 5, page 61) made it quite plain that neither confederation nor any new partnership of two states "through virgin birth" could be accepted, and that a federal solution meant a partnership of the two communities.[4] In January 2009, he emphasized the importance of human rights and fundamental freedoms for all Cypriots.[5] An ideal situation would be based on the following:

- compatibility of any settlement with the duties and rights of Cyprus and its people vis-à-vis the *acquis communautaire*; and, therefore,
- freedom of movement and of establishment on the whole island for all Cypriots;

- restitution of property stolen since 1974 to the legitimate owners and their heirs;
- a single government, parliament, and judicial system, free from the primitive ethno-linguistic-religious discrimination of former years, and conforming to the political and legal norms of the European Union;
- no discrimination, positive or negative;
- continuation of one republic with a single sovereignty, personality, and single citizenship, to enable a united Cyprus to speak with a single voice in the world;
- guarantees against unwarranted foreign interference, such as granting the right to individual countries to invade;
- withdrawal of foreign forces, in line with UN resolutions; and
- repatriation of illegal settlers, apart from special humanitarian cases.

This would in effect be a solution based on individual equality, with any form of discrimination being outlawed. Constitutional safeguards, in line with EU law, would be built in to protect the Greek-, Turkish-, Maronite-, and Armenian-Cypriot communities, to the extent that equality would prevail, whatever their religion or ethnic origin. A new constitution would have to be drafted and agreed, based, for example, on a French model, rather than on the divisive and unequal 1960 experiment. Those parts of the 1960 Constitution that have proven to be functional could of course be left intact. There would be no more apartheid, while everyone would have equal opportunity. It would, in fact, be rather like the United States or France, where there are various constitutional safeguards which protect minority communities but which do not officially discriminate, positively or negatively. Above all, it would conform to EU principles.

Anyone daring to seriously advocate such a solution would, of course, be dismissed by the self-interested partition-mongers as naive, eccentric, or even insane. And if the Cypriots agreed to this, Turkey, backed by the United States and Britain, would be likely to present obstacles, democratic though they purport to be. Thus, we are left with what, for want of a better word, we must term "reality." This means, literally, finding a solution that accommodates a concept of federalism, bizonalism, and bicommunalism on which the stakeholders can agree, and which allows people the right to their property and to decent European treatment. Most trickily, a solution should fall within the *acquis communautaire*. But, as we have seen from Annan V, Turkey and its strategic supporters fear a solution that complies with civilized European norms. However, the EU appears to be prepared to accept various derogations, while the Cyprus government is leaning over backwards to achieve a solution, even if it is not equitable. But the more the EU avoids its responsibilities, the more it erodes its founding principles and the *acquis communautaire*. Not only must woolly political concepts be accommodated, but also the military and territorial interests of the United States, Turkey, and Britain, which are not necessarily compatible with those of the EU. The British bases are not even part of the EU, while Cyprus and Britain are, an absurd and legally questionable anomaly and one of the causes of the curiously contrived package of treaties about which the Foreign Office itself was, as we have seen, so doubtful.

The partition-mongers' version of a solution means having to base a great deal of any putative agreement on the 1960 treaties with, of course, various derogations. Simply put, the problem is a constitutional, legal, social, and political maelstrom, where anachronisms have to be dressed in modern clothes to hide their inadequacies. Thus, we are left with having to find a compromise between EU principles and those of a more primitive era. We can console ourselves with the fact that nothing is perfect on Earth, and that one needs to be an artiste to fill the gap between perfection and reality. This is the challenge for those Cypriots who want to solve the problems with which the island has been burdened. These problems cannot be solved through disguised partition plans, such as Annan V, masquerading as federation. For a start, federations have a single foreign policy. The Annan scheme would have almost immediately led to deadlock, with Turkey trying to exploit the resulting tension to strengthen its strategic position and force itself into the EU.

"Federation" is certainly a useful concept within which to seek a solution, particularly since it can accommodate bizonality and bicommunalism, at least presentationally. Wherever it is cynically used as a word to disguise partition, or to further it, then, of course, it ceases to have meaning. To expect Cyprus to achieve a German style of federation would be to hope for too much. In Germany, there are of course no discriminatory constitutional ethno-national divisions, as in Cyprus's constitution. Nor are there in the United States. The Russian Federation is a good example of a huge country, indeed the world's largest, held together by a federal system. But comparing Cyprus to these countries is a faintly futile exercise, simply because Cyprus is small and compact. How does one compare the island with the republics and oblasts of Russia, the states of America and the *Länder* of Germany? With the word "confederation" matters can become yet more complicated, particularly if one takes the Swiss example, since the Swiss confederation is actually *less* federal in some ways than the bizonal, bicommunal solution envisaged for Cyprus.

One is bound to ask why the Greek- and Turkish-speaking people of the island were allocated discriminatory and divisive "job percentages" in the House of Representatives, police, civil service, and armed forces in the first place. The constitution was fodder for extremists and moderates alike, merely creating friction, particularly since it had not been worked out by the people who would have to live with it but imposed by outsiders on a "take it or leave it" basis. The divisive constitution has been a burden ever since, clashing with coherence. For example, for foreign policy to be coherent and in the hands of Cypriots, policy formulation and decision-making can only be achieved at a fully integrated level of government which leaves no room for a minority veto. Recruitment would need to be integrated, with competitive examinations in Greek or Turkish, and positions awarded on performance rather than religion and language. This works in other EU multi-lingual states, but then these countries do not suffer from the gross interference which has been Cyprus's lot. In any case, a system based on equality and merit is too democratic a solution for some external stakeholders and too much for the Turkish Cypriot leadership to grasp, let alone cope with, since they have spent so long in a self-imposed form of artificial occupation government. Thus, we are left with seeking a way to have a bizonal, bicommunal federation that has not only to be functional but also to conform with externally imposed constraints. This is because for some outsiders, the thought of Greek Cypriot and Turkish Cypriot agreement (difficult while Ankara keeps the Turkish Cypriots on a tight leash) is actually worrying, since it could affect the status of the U.S.-supported SBAs. To show the atavistic and anachronistic aspects, let us recall a Foreign Office view from 1964 which suggests that Britain was quite happy with, indeed preferred, a weak Cypriot state, to ensure the viability of the bases:

> The Cypriots and their supporters will be appealing to the concept of the sanctity of sovereignty and territorial integrity which has become something of a shibboleth at the UN. The argument can no doubt be extended to cover all foreign bases including the UK Sovereign Base Areas in Cyprus, which will be held to be an unnatural infringement of territorial integrity.[6]

This view epitomizes the hard-nosed attitude that prevails in international relations, at least when it comes to the sacred word "interests," interests which are not always spelt out but which one can broadly connect to control of resources through strategic and military means. Here, of course, Cyprus's location comes into its own. The eastern Mediterranean is simply too important to the United States and its Middle Eastern allies, and therefore Britain, for Cyprus to be let off the leash, particularly since Russia is reasserting its power in the region, not to forget French interests. Similarly to Cyprus, the United States will not let Britain off the leash vis-à-vis the bases. We have seen how Britain wished to both divest itself of the bases and escape from the Treaty of Guarantee, but succumbed to American pressure, essentially that of Kissinger. The geostrategic advantage to the United States of Britain having bases both in the eastern (Cyprus) and western (Gibraltar) Mediterranean is one that will not be easily relinquished, particularly since moral considerations are irrelevant, as the case of Diego Garcia so amply illustrates. Let us, therefore, look at the international factors which have tended to militate against a properly independent and united Cyprus, and which have therefore encouraged partition.

The Merry-Go-Round

Whatever the rights and wrongs of Cyprus's situation, the cold fact remains that the Middle Eastern interests of the United States are the order of the day. The hopes surrounding the much-heralded end of the Cold War have been dashed, and Cyprus bucked the euphoric trend of reunification and independence that became the fashion for a while. The lack of movement on the Cyprus problem illustrated that the ideology of the Cold War had been a mere excuse, disguising simple strategic interests which are, of course, still with us, especially in the eastern Mediterranean. The Cold War continues, albeit with different names and colors. If we add the atavistic human factors of pride, greed, ambition, and insecurity to the maelstrom, it is not difficult to understand why Cyprus is still divided and under illegal occupation. The reason is that, although not a member of NATO, Cyprus has to be its strategic Middle East instrument, both in the so-called war on terror and because it must not threaten Anglo-American policy. A Cyprus with its own independent foreign policy could not be guaranteed to toe the Anglo-American line on the Middle East, Iran, and Afghanistan, for example. The armchair strategists cannot cope with the realistic contention that a properly united and independent Cyprus could actually be a force for stability in the Middle East, in that it would not be beholden to any of the extremist forces in the eastern Mediterranean and would thus serve as an EU strongpoint. Memories of the independent-minded Makarios are still strong. Obviously, a neutral and demilitarized Cyprus is the answer. But the greed, pride, and ambition of the power-mongers get in the way. The logic of power rules over that of ethics in the diplomatic merry-go-round of the eastern Mediterranean, which is, in turn, so inextricably linked to the Middle, and, therefore, Greater Middle, East.

Microcosm of External Ambitions

Ever since Richard Coeur de Lion set foot on Cyprus, the island has been a strategic bone of contention of competing powers in a volatile region, becoming increasingly important as new powers emerged and flexed their muscles.[7] From being a focal point of Venetian-Ottoman rivalry, it then became an area of Anglo-French and then Anglo-Russian contention for control of the eastern Mediterranean. Britain always sided with the Ottomans in this equation. Today, it is a U.S./U.K.-Russian bone of contention, with the U.S./U.K. supporting the neo-Ottomans. We can certainly say, then, that since at least the Napoleonic Wars (the "Second World War"),[8] similar forces have competed around Cyprus, with the British gaining the upper hand in the Mediterranean and trying to keep Russian influence at bay by supporting the Ottomans. The United States then appeared as a powerful admixture after the Fourth World War, just as a reinvented Israel, imposed on the body of a vivisected Palestine, was consolidating its position and playing its part in the instability and war which has plagued the Middle East ever since. It is particularly significant that despite Cyprus's status as a cat's paw for so many years, it was only recently that the partition option was wheeled out as a tool for external powers to keep a finger in the pie. If such strong talk may appear irritating and even slightly insulting to some Cypriots, they can console themselves with the thought that Cyprus is but one of several cases of the disease of partition.

To the volatile and combustible cocktail of forces we can now add the European Union, although so far its power has been essentially economic ("soft" power in IR jargon) rather than military. Also, having no common foreign policy to speak of, the EU is divided between those who tend towards the U.S.-U.K. line (mainly the former Soviet satellites) and those of a more *communautaire* integrationist disposition, who are friendlier towards Russia. The end of the Cold War, or at least of the contrived and exaggerated ideological divide, has bequeathed up to now an intellectual void vis-à-vis understanding what the international system is, or whether it even exists, other than as a maelstrom of clashing interests, ideas, and formulas.

To understand Cyprus's situation, the nature of the problem, and what options are available to improve matters, one needs to see the linkage between NATO (mainly U.S.-run, with the UK as caddie and attendant) and EU defense aspirations. It is well enough known that the United States and Britain wish to use NATO as a worldwide policeman, as they are already doing in Afghanistan, and that an independent European army (rather than the NATO-connected ESDP arrangement) would pose a perceived threat to NATO in terms not only of influence but also in arms procurement. Apart from British and American opposition to a European force independent of NATO,[9] Britain has long feared French influence in Europe, which is one of the reasons that the British government could hardly bear the thought of sharing sovereignty with the French. Although Winston Churchill called for the creation of a European army "in which we would all bear a worthy and honourable part," he was in opposition at the time and seeking publicity for the next elections, which he had lost in 1945. When he returned to power, he backpeddled furiously, saying: "I meant it for them, not for us" and "we are with, but not of." Although Britain did eventually join the club, courtesy of the last of the British-European-Gaullist Mohicans, Edward Heath (the only British prime minister ever to have visited the Republic of Cyprus), its cooperative attitude was short-lived, dying with Heath's political demise in 1974 (unfortunately before the anti-Makarios coup). Britain never became a fully fledged member, and de Gaulle's prophesy that Britain would be a "worm in the apple" and an "American Trojan Horse" in Europe proved uncannily accurate, particularly in view of the Thatcher-Reagan relationship and Britain's clash with the Franco-German axis over the attack on, and invasion of, Iraq. Most importantly, one of the reasons why the United States and Britain supported EU enlargement so maniacally was to weaken both French power and the Franco-German axis. They also worked hard for the inclusion in NATO of the new EU members, as a way of weakening strictly EU military integration but also the authority of the UN. One important reason for the United States pushing for NATO enlargement is to "increase the Atlanticist voice in the new Europe."[10] One expert writes:

> The one entity with the capacity to challenge the United States in the near future is the European Union, if it were to become a tight federation with major military capabilities and if relations across the Atlantic were allowed to sour.[11]

To drive the nail home, in 2002 former British defense secretary Geoffrey Hoon—of Iraq fame—said: "NATO is and will be the only organisation for collective defence in Europe."[12] Understanding this background is necessary to see the constraints within which the Cyprus government is operating, and why the anti-integrationist members of the EU are also the more partitionist-minded. The EU's institutional future will determine the amount of leeway, or otherwise, that the Cyprus government will have in finding an equitable and functional solution.

Cyprus, the EU, Turkey, and NATO

It may perhaps appear hypocritical that while Britain and the United States frantically supported the prospective and new East European EU members' NATO applications, Cyprus somehow did not figure in the equation at all. Apart from Turkish opposition, Cypriot membership in NATO (even if Cyprus were to actively seek it) would be resisted by Britain and the United States to accommodate Turkish wishes. It is, after all, embarrassing enough having an EU member occupied by an alien country that wishes to join the (EU) club, part of which it is occupying. But it would be yet more embarrassing for a NATO member to be occupying a fellow member. The worst scenario for Turkey, Britain, and the United States would be a functional and functioning EU Common Foreign and Security Policy (CFSP), particularly with Cyprus as a member, since the common external defended border would make the Turkish occupation completely untenable, not only legally and morally, as at present, but also politically and militarily. If Turkey were to try and continue the occupation in such a scenario, it would not only disappear off the EU membership application screen but also come under constant pressure to stop flying over Greek islands, drop its territorial and maritime claims, and lift its threat of declaring war on Greece, if the latter exercises its right to implement its twelve-mile sea limits. The Cyprus problem and Turkey's claims on Greek territory are, of course, part and parcel of Greek-Turkish relations. Whenever there has been increased tension over Cyprus, Turkish jets and ships have encroached on Greek airspace. Were Greece and Turkey to agree on Cyprus, this would isolate and ridicule Turkey's aggressive claims on some Greek islands and airspace.[13] But thus far, Turkey will not talk turkey, preferring, rather, to continue to cement the division through illegal ethnic manipulation and force of arms. It has become increasingly obvious that Turkey is now using Cyprus as a hostage and bargaining chip in its application for EU membership. The United States and Britain condone this approach.[14]

Some mention of the United States' previous approach to Cyprus's efforts to join the EC is necessary at this point. Some EU countries, as well as the United States, had doubts about Cyprus joining the EU before a solution. However, as Turkish intransigence continued and the intercommunal talks remained bogged down, some began to see the prospect of EU membership as a way of contributing to a solution, believing that the mere prospect of membership would unite the island by default. But they did not reckon with Turkey's intransigent position on recognizing the occupied part as separate. As it grew increasingly obvious that Cyprus, the best qualified potential applicant out of the ten which were to be invited to join, could hardly be left out of the package, the United States turned to undermining Cyprus's application indirectly by referring to an application by both communities, thus throwing a wrench in the works, even though Cyprus's application was none of the United States' business. The State Department's special coordinator for Cyprus said in June 1990: "If there is going to be an application to the EC, then this must be a joint application of both communities."[15] In a brave response, Cyprus submitted its official application the following month. This, in turn, encouraged the United States and Britain to use the Cyprus problem to help Turkey's European aspirations, which, of course, also had the added advantage from their strategic viewpoint of weakening the EU; hence the Annan Plan. American and, more subtly, British pressure to admit Turkey was increasing exponentially. But at the EU's Copenhagen Summit in December 2002, the question of Turkish membership was deferred to the following December, while the EU statement made it quite clear that Cyprus would be admitted, whether or not there was a settlement. In a strong diplomatic slap in the face to the intrusive U.S. style of diplomacy, EU trade commissioner Pascal Lamy said: "It's certainly not up to the President of the United States to interfere in something so important and which mainly concerns Europeans."[16]

Despite the fact that Turkey is many years away, if ever, from proper EU membership, Britain and Turkey strongly support Turkish military involvement in European structures. Concomitantly, they oppose Cypriot, and to a lesser but more subtle extent, Greek military power in the eastern Mediterranean, since this upsets Turkey. The most blatant example of this was the S-300 crisis in 1998, when Turkey threatened to bomb the Russian anti-aircraft missiles if they were delivered to Cyprus for its defense against further Turkish attacks. In the end, Greece took the missiles.

In December 2001, as we have seen, Britain, the United States, and Turkey signed an agreement in Ankara, without an EU mandate, thus showing the irrelevance of a common EU position on defense matters. It attempted to guarantee Turkey a role in the then embryonic ERRF and to deny the force any role in the eastern Aegean or around Cyprus. This confused matters. Turkey had been holding NATO to ransom by refusing to release NATO assets for use in the ERRF. Its basic position was—and is—that Cyprus must not be a member of any European defense force, whether that force is independent of, or dependent on, NATO.

The rather obvious reason for all this palaver was that any role for Cyprus, even if only symbolic, would have strengthened the Greece-Cyprus defense doctrine, thus weakening, from Turkey's perspective, its position on Cyprus and its territorial claims. Protracted negotiations took place, after which the EU agreed to keep Cyprus out of European military operations in the area, thus weakening the EU's already battered reputation as an independent entity. Greek pressure intensified, ensuring an addition to the British-U.S.-Turkish paper, stipulating that no NATO member would threaten the use of, or use, force against an EU member. On the question of its own participation, Turkey had to back down, being offered an indefinable consultative role. Despite the frenetic diplomacy surrounding the whole shenanigans and the appearance of an agreement, Turkey in fact continues to threaten Greece with war over Greece's sea limits, and its parliament has not lifted its *casus belli* in the case that Greece extend its limits to twelve miles, as it is entitled to do. Turkey's position is untenable since, although it has not signed the UN Law of the Sea Convention, as Greece has, it itself nevertheless exercises a twelve-mile limit in the Black Sea. The Turkish situation is, then, not clear-cut, and exercises a destabilizing influence. The following maxim comes to mind when considering U.S.-British-NATO policy in the eastern Mediterranean, but particularly over Cyprus: it is easier to confuse in order to control, than to control in order to confuse: power without responsibility is easier than responsibility without power.[17]

Britain and America have exploited the Cyprus problem to weaken European integration, particularly on the military front. In this sense, Cyprus has provided collateral benefits to the United States and its British aide-de-camp. Cyprus is constrained by being torn between an Anglo-American NATO, on the one hand, and a germinating CFSP, on the other. This conflict of interests explains why Turkey is still being allowed to use Cyprus as a hostage to gain entry into the EU. Turkish behavior has, however, irritated leading European politicians. For example, when the United States was applying intense pressure on the EU in 2002/3 (see above, 88-89) to open accession talks with Turkey, the EU trade commissioner commented:

> It's a classic case of US diplomacy to want to put Turkey in Europe. The further the boundaries of Europe extend, the better US interests are secured. Can you imagine the reaction if we told them that they had to enlarge into Mexico?[18]

More recently, the political, cultural, and psychological divide between Turkey and the EU became more pronounced when Turkey threatened to veto the appointment of the Danish prime minister as NATO secretary general (see above, 79-80), on the grounds that Denmark had a Kurdish-language broadcasting station and that Danish newspapers had published cartoons lampooning Mohammed. The Turkish threat was in fact simply a ploy to gain more NATO positions. The French foreign minister was particularly critical of Turkey's intemperate behavior, while an expert wrote:

> It is a question of Turkey trying to impose its Islamist and chauvinist policies on another European state—and indeed on the whole NATO alliance. And if this is how it behaves before it has been admitted to the European Union, has it not invited us all to guess how it would behave when it had a veto power in those councils? . . . Turkey wants all the privileges of NATO and EU membership but also wishes to continue occupying Cyprus, denying Kurdish rights and lying about the Armenian genocide.[19]

By this stage in our book, the causes of, and reasons behind, the unseemly division of Cyprus and the current condoning of aggression by certain powers should be clear enough. Let us finish by looking at the strengths, weaknesses, opportunities, and threats regarding Cyprus's international position, the so-called "SWOT" analysis, primarily used for business plans but no less apt for the Cyprus business at hand.

Strengths

Cyprus's strongest card is its membership in the EU, reinforced in turn by its membership in the euro. For those who are cynical about the EU's power and/or willingness to help Cyprus, it is worth recalling that Cyprus gained membership despite virulent opposition from Turkey. The rejection of Annan V was also, it needs to be remembered, taken on the plan's own merits and demerits, since the EU had already unlinked Cyprus's membership from a solution. Although there had been some dissenting voices in some countries, for example in the Netherlands, the European Commission proved stronger than these disparate, nationally based noises. The diplomacy that saw Cyprus joining on one ticket, with nine other members, was an enormous advantage, since any last-minute attempt to link Cyprus's membership to acceptance of the Annan scheme would have been squashed by a Greek threat to veto the whole mass-membership package. A small country with a third of its territory under occupation by NATO's second largest army, and with two hundred thousand of its inhabitants forcefully displaced, had met the tough accession criteria. Accession has acted as a catalyst for reunification within an EU context, rather than one based on the intrusive and aggressive politics of the nineteenth and twentieth centuries. The role of the EU as a force for international stability and that of Cyprus as a strongpoint of eastern Mediterranean and Middle Eastern stability are clearly mutually enhancing.

The European project is a long and sometimes tortuous road, with all sorts of traps along the way, one of them, paradoxically, being democracy: French, Dutch, and Irish voters have shown this in no uncertain terms in their rejection of the constitution. But the project continues, albeit slowly, with hiccups, but ineluctably, like a tortoise. It is vital that the Cyprus government remain as *communautaire* as possible. The next hurdle is the Schengen Agreement, currently complicated for Cyprus because of both the occupation and the status of the British territories. It is equally vital that Cyprus become a full participant in the CFSP, when it eventually begins to operate seriously, if necessary by taking the question to the European Court of Justice. Even if a future Cyprus is demilitarized, the right of participation in the CFSP should still remain. Non-members should have no *locus standi* whatsoever on Cyprus's rights as an EU member. On another tack, and given the possibility of a two-track Europe owing to the non-*communautaire* attitude of some of the ex-Soviet satellites such as Poland and the Czech Republic, Cyprus needs to ensure that it remains in core Europe, and not on a putative future fringe. Its stoic people have worked too hard, and suffered too much, for selfish external interests to be able to dictate what Cyprus can and cannot do within the EU. It is for the EU alone to decide on whatever temporary derogations may be necessary for Cyprus. It is well known that, for better or worse, horse trading tends to be part of the Council of Ministers' meetings. Cyprus merely needs to be aware of its rights, so as not to end up as a political football.

Another clear strength is Cyprus's economy: of the twelve most recent EU members, Cyprus has the highest GDP per capita and a robust economy. The very fact that it survived a brutal invasion and continuing occupation, which degraded some of the most effective parts of its economy at the time, bears ample testimony to the resilient nature of the island's population. Significant for its long-term economic prospects is the fact that Cyprus spends more than the EU *per capita* average on education. Perhaps somewhat perversely, the Turkish-inflicted blackening of the economy of occupied northern

Cyprus is an advertisement that the occupier and the illegals should get out and let the Turkish Cypriots develop their economy by reuniting with their Greek Cypriot compatriots.

A particular strength is Cyprus's geographical position. Although this has proven historically to be a disadvantage for its inhabitants, an equitable solution, free from foreign interference, would enhance its value as an important point of stability in EU and UN humanitarian operations, in which it would serve as a bridge of peace in the area, and even as an independent third party in resolving conflicts. Its humanitarian role during the Israeli invasion of Lebanon in the summer of 2007 is an example.

Yet another strength, but more of a tactical tool, is Cyprus's membership in the British Commonwealth. As we have seen, Britain would immediately go to Australia's or New Zealand's assistance if they were threatened, while expediency ruled when Cyprus was invaded. Nevertheless, Cyprus needs to exploit its membership to the full. It is significant that many Commonwealth countries have shared experiences of the problems caused by colonial and post-colonial policies that still dog the world.

Weaknesses

The most obvious weaknesses are the divisive elements of the 1960 package which continue to haunt any attempt to arrive at a democratic, functional solution in line with EU membership. While it is true that free Cyprus easily meets the criteria of an advanced liberal democracy, the same can obviously not be said for the occupied zone. Unless the Cypriots themselves can agree to "reconstitute the constitution" in a genuinely reunified Cyprus, a half-way house will continue to muddy the legal, political, and social waters. The only external force currently involved with the power to help to achieve a bi-communal and bizonal solution in conformity with modern democratic norms is the EU itself. But until the EU shows itself more willing to help achieve a fully functional solution, the 1960 arrangement will continue to exert its baleful and undermining influence, simply because few have yet dared to speak out openly and denounce it for what it is.

A connected weakness, which of course relates directly to 1960, is Cyprus's military value: if it were not for the British bases and electronic spying posts, the United States would never even have become involved, at least not to the same extent. As a result of its involvement, the United States now enjoys, apart from its echelon partnership with Britain, its own listening posts in occupied Cyprus. It goes almost without saying that the Turkish government strongly supports the existence of the bases, simply because they underline Cyprus's perceived importance as a military staging area for the Middle East, and because by supporting their existence, they gain U.S. and U.K. support for their occupation and partition of the island.

Another weakness is the difficulty of Cyprus's participation in the above-mentioned Schengen Agreement. Again, it is for the EU to help the Cyprus government in its representations about the border problems. Since the government of Cyprus is responsible for the international borders of the whole island but cannot exercise its rights in the occupied zone, the EU needs to emphasize that the area of Cyprus that does not currently operate under the *acquis communautaire* is also invalid for Schengen purposes, while making a statement that the internal barrier imposed by the Turkish army means that the Schengen Agreement is only valid up to the illegal occupation line, pending a solution.   In the meantime, the Cyprus government could pass a law stipulating that the Schengen Agreement can only be valid for unoccupied Cyprus, until the *acquis communautaire* becomes valid throughout the whole island. There is of course a distant parallel here with the case of the (West) German Basic Law (a *de facto* constitution), so called because of the division of Germany.

Connected to the above is Cyprus's right to membership in various international organizations of which Turkey is a member, but which Cyprus has not been able to join, owing to Turkish vetoes. Here again, Cyprus needs to exploit its membership in the EU to gain the support it needs, not always easy, since Britain, on behalf of the United States, tends to subtly support the Turkish position at EU meetings.

Opportunities

Clearly, EU membership is the essential opportunity, just as it is a strength. Simply being a member *per se* reinforces the illegality and political absurdity of the occupation and partition of an EU member state, at the hands of an applicant, into the bargain. Therefore, unless the EU disappears, Cyprus's international position is strengthening day by day, to the obvious weakening of Turkey's *locus standi*. The enormous extent of this major "free" advantage may not be immediately apparent to Cypriot policymakers, simply because of the tense day-to-day activity of dealing with the Cyprus problem in international fora which tends to make it difficult to stand back dispassionately and to capitalize on obvious advantages. Another major trump card is Cyprus's membership in the Council of Europe, where Turkey has quite rightly been humiliated on many occasions by the ECHR, and will continue to be, as long as it persists with its occupation of a fellow council member.

Threats

The Cypriots in the free part of the island live under a sword of Damocles, one of further invasion. This is combined with a strange sense of boredom and cynicism at having had to wait so long to return to the homes and businesses from which they were torn, while still not knowing the fate of fourteen hundred Greek Cypriots taken into captivity by the Turkish army in 1974. The Turkish Cypriots, many of whom are not even descended from ethnic Selçuk or Osmanli Turks, live under the sword of uncertainty and of being marginalized through a major and continuing act of ethnic manipulation perpetrated by an alien government, occupying forces, and quisling collaborators. A major threat, then, is EU inaction, for the simple historical reason that inaction can become malignant and be exploited, thereby leading to extremism and violence. The United States and Britain will currently be frantically casting around for ways to play down the embarrassment to Turkey because of the Republic of Cyprus being host to its European partners for six months when it assumes the EU presidency in 2012, while an illegal administration and the Turkish military and government, who want to join the EU, look on. The worst scenario would be for Turkey to manufacture various incidents, accompanied by threats either against free Cyprus or Greece itself, as happens whenever there is tension over Cyprus, and for a further attack on Cyprus, or another but bigger Imia-type incident, to distract attention from Turkey's embarrassment. It is well known that whenever it has domestic problems, Turkey tends to whip up nationalist fervor, usually against Greece. Turkey is not alone in this: just as the invasion of the Malvinas/Falklands was a useful distraction from the Argentine military junta's problems, so was Thatcher's "war first" response useful in winning the next elections. Foreign policy can actually be predictable and almost childish when it comes to proud machismo, or, in the case of Thatcher, proud "feminismo."

Connected to the above, a possible threat may be lurking in the current tendency of the United States and Britain to continually withhold criticism of Turkish behavior toward Cyprus (notwithstanding the private FCO views that we have seen earlier), and the United States' keenness to support Turkish strategic aims, despite their destabilizing effects. One area of concern is the appointment of Philip Gordon as assistant secretary of state for European affairs in the Obama government. As we have seen in chapter 5, as early as 1997, Gordon was arguing that "formal partition would be no worse than the current situation."[20] Five years later, he ended an article, written with a well-known advocate of official Turkish positions, thus:

> An agreement by the two Cypriot communities to live together in a bi-national state that would join the EU in 2004 remains the best solution to the Cyprus problem. But in diplomacy, optimal solutions are rarely available. Deferring the unification of Cyprus until Turkey is also in a position to join the Union is far preferable to the regional crisis that, in the absence of intense American engagement, will almost certainly occur.[21]

The term used above, "bi-national state," is about as far as one can get without talking about two states. One is left wondering whether the authors mean two states in one or one state in two, neither of which are possible in terms of having a single international personality. The language is expressly obfuscator, yet to the point of appearing naive, since the term lacks any precise meaning. The obvious question arises as to how such a state could possibly have, for example, a single foreign policy, let alone fulfill the *acquis communautaire*. Yet more naively, the authors seem to think that this dysfunctional state would not be allowed to join the EU until "Turkey was in a position to join," thereby making a mockery of the idea of a sovereign state in the first place, and revealing the cynical view that Turkey should use Cyprus as a ransom to gain entry to the E.U. By default, they typify the armchair strategists who have for so long used Cyprus as a tool for their own countries' interests, with no regard for the interests of the actual inhabitants whom they affect. In the end, their hopeful prognostications were exposed as wishful thinking, since a "bi-national state" did not join the E.U. Rather, a single state was able to join, despite being occupied. In another bizarre gaffe, and betraying their cynical use of Cyprus's occupation to promote Turkey's EU aspirations, Gordon and his co-author wrote in another article: "Technically, resolution of the island's 30-year-old division is not a prerequisite for Turkey's EU membership."[22] At the time they wrote their article, not only had the EU made it plain that a solution to the Cyprus problem would not be a precondition for membership, but Cyprus had also already signed the accession treaty. Turkey, however, has continued to refuse to recognize the republic, thereby displaying a lack of respect for the E.U. By implying that Turkey could join the EU while occupying part of it, the authors were insulting people's intelligence and assuming their complete ignorance.

If NATO, in the guise of the United States and Britain, really wishes to keep Russia from becoming more directly involved in Cyprus than hitherto, then one obvious way would be to stop trying to strong-arm the legal government of Cyprus to agree to recognize an illegal occupation and partition as the price for a solution, when in fact such a scenario could only lead to further strife and the possible takeover of the whole island. Such a dark scenario would suit Russia, given the almost immediate disemboweling of NATO's soft underbelly by Greece's withdrawal from NATO and possible bombing of the Bosporus that would occur if Turkey attacked free Cyprus. Lest anyone consider such a scenario an impossible and irresponsible exaggeration, then he should ask himself whether anybody predicting a Turkish invasion in 1964 or 1974 was considered stupid. Even if Greece were not to respond militarily, NATO would still be massively weakened.

Thus, it appears that the most responsible solution is for Britain and the United States to work rather harder at persuading Turkey to cease its forced partition of Cyprus, and for the Cyprus government to work with Russia to ensure the demilitarization of Cyprus, perhaps initially through direct methods, such as naval visits, to show their right to independence in foreign policy. In a negotiated solution, the Cyprus government could then balance British against Russian strategic interests, thus encouraging demilitarization and EU strategic support. It is, after all, American interest in the British bases that has dictated American and British pro-Turkish policy. If Britain were to have the courage to withdraw, as it attempted to, this would create more stability in the eastern Mediterranean, and therefore in the Middle East.

Conclusions

Cyprus's fate can only be comprehended within the context of the interests of NATO, the EU, and Turkey. Up to now, the powers involved in Cyprus have kept their heads in the sand, while Turkey has continued to artificially and illegally consolidate its occupation through the systematic destruction of the Turkish Cypriot community and its replacement by illegal settlers. At the same time, the European Union has painfully and slowly, but nevertheless steadily, improved its institutional strength, which can but stand Cyprus in good stead for a just solution for the island. This would be predicated on a reversal of ethnic manipulation and based on European law. Such an approach would hopefully put an end to the manufactured fear, misplaced pride, selfish interests, and jejune macho power politics that should no longer have a place in the Europe of today, or even the world. Let us end this chapter with a particularly pertinent and perspicacious quote by the British high commissioner to Cyprus in 1971: "While the situation is not at this moment getting worse, the potential for evil increases the longer the communities remain apart."[23]

CHAPTER EIGHT

In Conclusion

To ignore history is to ignore the wolf at the door.[1]

LET US first remind ourselves what this book has set out to do: to question partition as a solution to international relations problems, and to show it to be an intellectually inadequate and morally expedient approach to peace, and one that creates more problems than it solves. This is particularly true in the case of Cyprus, where partition as a systematic policy, applied late in human history, has been shown to be divisive in the worst sense of the term, and merely a cover for brutality and selfishness. Concurrently, the book has also tried to show that the term "partition" is itself sufficiently ambivalent and in some cases even quasi-respectable as to defy common sense, and that in the case of Cyprus, we are simply talking about partition as a dishonest euphemism for invasion, occupation, massive violations of human rights, ethnic cleansing, substitution of population (illegal colonization), name-changing, destruction of culture, and common theft, which no amount of pseudo bonhommie-type diplomatic backslapping can solve. The book then went on to cut through the jargon of the weak side of international relations theory and think-tankery to confront the problem of Cyprus's situation in as clear a way as possible, after which it set out, analyzed, and evaluated the historical underpinning so vital to understanding the origins and, therefore, the nature of the current problem. We said that partition had never even reared its ugly head through hundreds of years of Frankish, Venetian, and Ottoman possession of Cyprus, and that it was only with the arrival of "divide and rule" methods of governing that the people of Cyprus began to feel that it was time to fight for freedom. Bringing the young and unstable state of Turkey into the Cyprus problem in breach of the Treaty of Lausanne only exacerbated the problem, concurrently creating major problems between Greece and Turkey which remain to the present, along with the Cyprus problem, which has become a permanent feature of Greek-Turkish relations. The book demonstrated how unstable and divisive the 1960 arrangement was, as well as being legally questionable, and how it was in itself a recipe (whether expressly or otherwise being a moot point) for division. This led to a major crisis when, on Britain's advice, the president of Cyprus tried to amend the constitution, and to the involvement of the UN (to Turkish anger). The Turkish rejection of the

97

moderate and anti-partitionist Plaza Report then led to a malevolent stasis, which in turn led to the crisis of 1967, which proved to be a kind of rehearsal for the invasion of 1974, which is still with us, with its baggage of continuing occupation, ethnic cleansing, and demographic manipulation.

The book then turned to a brief but necessary autopsy of the discredited "Annan Plan," which was a last minute flurry of additions to the more painstakingly worked out, but nevertheless contrived, plan introduced in 2002, as a way of ensuring that Cyprus would be united when it joined the EU. When it turned out that the scheme was little more than a reshuffling of the iffy 1960 package, with the added "attraction" of legalizing the occupation and much of the ethnic cleansing and manipulation, which could have resulted in disagreement and further partition, it was rejected by the people of Cyprus. The lesson learned was to beware disguised partition plans.

Then we looked at various cases of partition, juxtaposing and comparing them with Cyprus, concluding that the history of partition is indeed a dismal one, whether considering India, Palestine or, for example, Ireland, where only recently, two soldiers and a policeman were shot dead by those seeking the reunification of Ireland, a story that goes back at least to 1921. This led to deeper considerations of the arguments about partition in Cyprus, where the book dealt with the European, legal, moral, economic, political, and practical aspects. This analysis was followed by a rebuffal of the "isolation myth" invented to suggest that the Turkish Cypriots are somehow victims of Greek Cypriot policies and to draw the world's attention away from the fact that Turkey is illegally occupying another sovereign state and indulging in an orgy of demographic manipulation. The section showed that the Turkish Cypriots are themselves victims of Turkish policies, but that, thanks to the help of the Cyprus government, they enjoy many of the rights of their Greek Cypriot compatriots and, in many cases, more. This took us to the above chapter, in which we have looked at the idea of federation, warned against using the word dishonestly as a backdoor way to further divide the island, emphasized the importance of functionality, considered Cyprus as a microcosm surrounded by poker players spitting out their fingernails of ambition onto the island, and looked at the strengths, weaknesses, opportunities, and threats.

It remains only to emphasize that a genuine federation, agreed since 1977 and confirmed in numerous UN resolutions since then, is the only viable and functional solution for Cyprus, and that this can only be achieved without the malign, damaging, and self-interested meddling of outside powers, without reverting to anachronistic and obsolete treaties that constitute the historical cause of the whole problem. It is only within the framework of the European Union that a lasting solution can be achieved, one that ensures that all Cypriot citizens will enjoy the full benefits of EU membership. The EU, for its part and for its own self-respect, must insist that a solution falls within its legal, political, economic, and social parameters. Not to do so will weaken the very basis of its existence. In this sense, Cyprus is a veritable gauge of the future of the EU. We end with a quote from the Plaza Report which, had it been heeded in 1965, would have rendered the need for this book unnecessary:

If the purpose of a settlement of the Cyprus question is to be the preservation rather than the destruction of the state and if it is to foster rather than militate against the development of a peacefully united people, I cannot help wondering whether the physical division of the minority from the majority should not be considered a desperate step in the wrong direction.

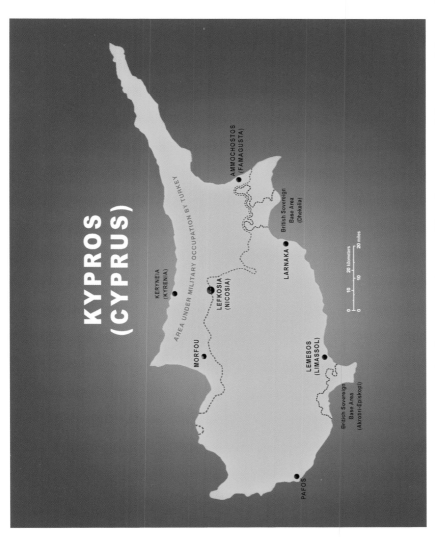

Map showing the 1974 UN cease-fire line across the Republic of Cyprus, and the area of the republic under military occupation by Turkey

(Courtesy of the Press and Information Office, Republic of Cyprus)

Map of the European Union that includes Cyprus
(Courtesy of the European Commission)

NOTES

Introduction

1.   Harold Nicolson, *Peacemaking 1919*, Universal Library Edition, no. 178 (New York: Grosset and Dunlap, 1965), 207.

2.   House of Commons, Foreign Affairs Committee, *Cyprus* (London: HMSO, 1987), xii, quoted in Alan James, "The UN Force in Cyprus," *International Affairs* 65, no. 3 (Royal Institute of International Affairs, London, summer 1989): 482.

3.   "Turkish Land Grab in Cyprus," editorial, *New York Times*, 16 November 1983.

4.   For a piercing look at Turkey's objectives, see Christos P. Ioannides, *In Turkey's Image: The Transformation of Occupied Cyprus into a Turkish Province* (New Rochelle, N.Y.: Aristides T. Caratzas, 1991).

5.   Secretary of State for Foreign Affairs, memorandum, 3 September 1955, CAB 129/77.

6.   Christopher Hitchens, *Hostage to History* (London and New York: Verso, 1997), 112.

7.   Ahmet Gürkan, *Kipris Postasi*, 20 December 1983.

8.   Ioannides, *In Turkey's Image*, 155.

9.   See Radha Kumar, "The Troubled History of Partition," *Foreign Affairs* 76, no. 1 (Washington, January/February 1997): 29, where she writes: "The conflict following independence in 1960 was compounded by the fact that Turkey, Greece and Britain were appointed protecting powers by the constitution. The formal structure this gave to a wider engagement in the conflict drew both the Greek and Turkish armies in and permitted international acceptance of Turkey's invasion in 1974 and what was until then a de facto partition."

10.   Michael A. Zachariades, "Transplanted Populations and the Problems Caused: Cyprus" (Leiden University, September 2002, at www.hellenism.net and www.aunitedcyprus.com).

11.   *American Foreign Policy: Current Documents, 1983* (Washington, D.C.: Department of State, 1985), 472, quoted in Marios Evriviades, "The United States Strategic Interests and the Policy of Partition," in *The United States and Cyprus: Double Standards and the Rule of Law* (Washington, D.C.: American Hellenic Institute Foundation, Inc., 2002). Evriviades analyses how Congress' efforts to deprive Turkey of some of its military grants in the

wake of the illegal declaration of the "TRNC" were scotched by Assistant Secretary of Defense Richard Perle.

12.   Christopher Hitchens, "What's Wrong with Partition," *The New Statesman*, London, 21 August 1997.

Chapter One

1.   For a most interesting discussion about partition, see Brendan O'Leary, "Analysing Partition: Definition, Classification and Explanation," *MFPP Working Paper*, no. 27 (Institute for British-Irish Studies, Geary Institute for the Social Sciences, University College, Dublin, and Institute of Governance, Centre for International Borders Research, Queen's University, Belfast, 2006). Also printed as IBIS working paper no. 77.

2.   Martin Wight, "Why Is There No International Theory?" in *Diplomatic Investigations*, ed. Herbert Butterfield and Martin Wight (London: George Allen and Unwin Ltd., 1966), 17-34.

3.   Ibid., 17.

4.   See, for example, Madeleine Albright, "The Testing of American Foreign Policy," *Foreign Affairs* 77, no. 6 (Washington, D.C., November/December 1998): 50-64; Condoleeza Rice, "Promoting the National Interest," *Foreign Affairs* 79, no. 1 (2000): 45-62; and Robert B. Zoellick, "A Republican Foreign Policy," ibid., 63-78.

5.   Marc Weller, "The Rambouillet Conference on Kosovo," *International Affairs* 75, no. 2 (Royal Institute of International Affairs, London, April 1999): 211-51.

6.   For a thorough look at the dichotomy of international relations theory and political science, on the one hand, and the exacting study of history and its benefits, on the other, using Cyprus as a case study, see William Mallinson, *Cyprus: Diplomatic History and the Clash of Theories in International Relations* (London and New York: I. B. Tauris, forthcoming).

7.   Lin Yutang, *The Importance of Living* (1938; London: Heinemann, 1976), 404.

8.   *The Times Atlas of the World*, ref. ed. (London: Times Books, 2003), 22.

9.   A. J. P. Taylor, *The Struggle for the Mastery of Europe, 1848–1918* (1954; Oxford University Press, 1991), 250; see also Robert Stevens, *Cyprus, A Place of Arms: Power Politics and Ethnic Conflict in the Eastern Mediterranean* (London: Pall Mall, 1966).

10.   Spyros Litsas, "The Origins of the Enosis Question in Cyprus," *Defensor Pacis* 17 (Athens, July 2005): 123, quoted in B. E. Buckle, *The Life of Benjamin Disraeli, Earl of Beaconsfield* (London, 1920), 6:291; see also Dwight E. Lee, *Great Britain and the Cyprus Convention of 1878* (Cambridge, Mass.: Harvard University Press, 1934).

11.   Southern European Department to Minister of State, 27 October 1976, FCO 9/2388, file WSC 023/1, pt. H, memorandum, in William Mallinson, "1976: British Cyprus and the Consolidation of American Desires in the Eastern Mediterranean," *Defensor Pacis* 21 (Athens, September 2007).

12.   FCO, "British Policy on Cyprus: July to September 1974," paper, 14 January 1976, FCO 9/2379, file WSC/548/1.

13.   Henry Kissinger, *Nuclear Weapons and Foreign Policy* (New York: Harper and Brothers, 1957), 165.

14.   South East European Department, FCO, "British Interests in the Eastern Mediterranean," 11 April 1975, paper, FCO 46/1248, file DPI/516/1, in William Mallinson, "The Year After: Cyprus and the Shipwrecking of British Sovereignty," *Defensor Pacis* 18 (Athens, July 2006).

15.   David Leigh and Richard Norton-Taylor, "We are now a Client State," *The Guardian*, 17 July 2003.

16.   F. Davies, letter in *Daily Mail*, 7 January 2009.

17.   FCO meeting, 6 January 1972, record, FCO 9/1527, file WSG/548/3.

18.   Mottershead to PUS, letter enclosing brief for Defence and Overseas (Official) Committee, 27 April 1964, FO 371/29840, in William Mallinson, *Cyprus, a Modern History*, rev. ed. (London and New York: I. B. Tauris, 2009), 38.

19.   Perceval to Fort, letter, 29 July 1976, FCO 9/2386, file WSC 023/1, pt. F.

20.   Christopher Hill, *The Changing Politics of Foreign Policy* (Basingstoke: Palgrave Macmillan, 2003), 168-69.

21.   The word "janissary" derives from *yeni çeri*, which means "new soldier" in Turkish. They were children taken by the Ottomans to be brought up as the élite guards of the sultan. Most were Greek and Balkan children.

22.   An enormous number of books have, of course, been written about the Balkans. This author found the following particularly useful: Misha Glenny, *The Balkans 1804–1999* (London: Granta Books, 1999); L. S. Stavrianos, *The Balkans since 1453* (1958; London: C. Hurst and Co., 2000); and Rebecca West [Cecily Fairfield], *Black Lamb and Grey Falcon* (Macmillan London Ltd., 1942; Edinburgh: Canongate Classics, 1993).

23.   The French, of course, have the expression "filer à l'anglaise."

24.   Thomas E. Hachey, *The Problem of Partition: Peril to World Peace* (Chicago: Rand McNally College Publishing Company, 1972).

25.   Brendan O'Leary, "Debating Partition: Justifications and Critiques," *MFPP Working Paper*, no. 28 (Institute for British-Irish Studies, University College, Dublin and Institute of Governance, Centre for International Borders Research, Queen's University, Belfast, 2006). Also printed as IBIS working paper no. 78.

Chapter Two

1.   Kirkpatrick to Nutting, 26 June 1955, Memorandum, FO 371/17640, file RG-1081/535, cited in Mallinson, *Cyprus, a Modern History*, 24.

2.   Taylor, *The Struggle for the Mastery of Europe*, 60.

3.   See Reed Coughlan, *Enosis and the British: British Official Documents 1878–1950*, vol. 11 of *Sources for the History of Cyprus*, ed. Paul W. Wallace and Andreas G. Orphanides (Altamont, N.Y.: Greece and Cyprus Research Center, 2004).

4.   "Tyranny with Hypocrisy," *Evagoras*, 11–24 October 1901; and Coughlan, *Enosis and the British*, 27-30.

5.   Ibid.

6.   Bolton (Commissioner, Cyprus) to Secretary of State for the Colonies, letter, 2 June 1912, in Coughlan, *Enosis and the British*, 34.

7.   Arnold Toynbee, "Cyprus, the British Empire and Greece," in *Survey of International Affairs* (London: Oxford University Press and Humphrey Milford, 1931), 354-94.

8.   Arnold Toynbee, "Cyprus," *New Statesman and Nation*, 23 April 1932, in Coughlan, *Enosis and the British*, 173.

9.   Robert Holland, *Britain and the Revolt in Cyprus, 1954–1959* (Oxford University Press, 1998), 13. Holland does not, however, give his source. It is surprising that the publisher did not pick up on this.

10.   Mallinson, *Cyprus, A Modern History*, 12-13, FO 371/48281, file R-16249/4/19.

11.   Ibid.

12.   William Mallinson, "Turkish Invasions, Cyprus and the Treaty of Guarantee," *Synthesis-Review of Modern Greek Studies* 3, no. 1 (London School of Economics and Political Science, 1999): 41, FO 371/67084, file R-13462/G.

13.   Mallinson, *Cyprus, A Modern History*, 14.

14.   John Peck, *Internal Foreign Office paper on Cyprus*, 22 December 1947, FO 371/67084, file R-1683/8/G.

15.   Secretary of State for the Colonies, July 1954, CAB 129/69.

16.   Report on Cyprus, Agenda, Ninth Session of the General Assembly of the United Nations, New York, 23–24 September 1954, FO 953/1964, file G-11926/20.

17.   Bowker to Young, 15 February 1955, letter, FO 371/117625, file RG 1081/120.

18.   Cox to Fisher, 13 July 1956, letter, FO 953/1694, file G 11926/23.

19.   Governor of Cyprus to Secretary of State for Colonies, 12 August 1955, letter, FO 371/117652, file RG-1081/900.

20.   Brendan O'Malley and Ian Craig, *The Cyprus Conspiracy* (London and New York: I. B. Tauris, 1999), 21.

21.   Mallinson, *Cyprus, A Modern History*, 28.

22.   William Mallinson, *Portrait of an Ambassador: The Life, Times and Writings of Themistocles Chrysanthopoulos* (Athens: The American College of Greece, 1998), 27.

23.   Prime Minister's Private Secretary to Rumbold, 17 July 1955, letter, FO 371/117644, file RG-1081/692.

24.   Butterworth (State Department), 10 August 1955, telegram, FRUS 1955–1957, 24:277.

25.   Holland, *Britain and the Revolt in Cyprus*, 69; see also Speros Vryonis, *The Mechanism of Catastrophe: The Turkish Pogrom of 6–7 September 1955 and the Destruction of the Greek Community of Istanbul* (New York: Greekworks.com, 2005).

26.   Peter Wright, *Spycatcher* (New York: Viking Penguin Inc., 1987), 154.

27.   Holmes to Secretary of State, 30 July 1956, memorandum, FRUS 1955–1957, 24:389-93.

28.   Glass to Fletcher-Cooke, 9 August 1956, letter, FO 953/1695, file PG 11926/50.

29.   Hitchens, *Hostage to History*, 45-47.

30.   Stella Soulioti, *Fettered Independence: Cyprus, 1878–1964*, Minnesota Mediterranean and East European Monographs, no. 16 (Minneapolis: University of Minnesota, Modern Greek Studies, 2006), 1:36-40.

31.   Ibid., 55-57.   In 1984, Denktash admitted that a friend of his had planted the bomb.   Kutlu Adali, a brave Turkish Cypriot journalist, wrote about it on 14 July, in the *Ortam* newspaper.   Twelve years later, he was murdered, almost certainly by "deep state" Turkish extremists connected to the military and the dirty side of big business.   See Hitchens, *Hostage to History*, 4; and idem, "The 'Green Line' Fallacy," *The Nation*, 30 December 1996.   Of particular interest is the fact that Adali's wife recently stated that her husband was murdered after he had criticized a senior Turkish general for corruption.   In 2005, the European Court of Human Rights decided that the investigation following the murder was inadequate and fined the Turkish government €95,000, including €20,000 for Adali's wife.   See Zaman, 16 March 2009, at www.todayszaman.com.

32.   Soulioti, *Fettered Independence*, 1:56.   She quotes from a 1984 Granada Television documentary, "End of Empire."   See also Stavros A. Panteli, *History of Cyprus* (London: East-West Publications, 2000), 361, where he gives the figure of 109 killed.

33.   Hugh Foot, *A Start in Freedom* (London: Hodder and Stoughton, Ltd., 1964), 150.

34.   British Ambassador, Athens, to Secretary of State, 16 January 1959, *Annual Review for 1958*, FO 371/144516, file RG-1011/1.

35.   Tassos Papadopoulos, speech, seminar, Carnegie Endowment in Diplomacy, 4 August 1969, published as *Cyprus, Developments and Realities* (Nicosia: Zavallis Press, 1969).

36.   Soulioti, *Fettered Independence*, 1:205-6.

37.   Secondé to Ramsbotham, 11 March 1971, letter, FCO 9/1353, file WSC 1/1.

38.   Costas Yennaris, *From the East* (London: Elliott and Thompson Ltd., 2003), 68.   Part of Zorlu's speech at the fateful 1955 London conference.

39.   Ibid., 69.

40.   By which is meant "Turkish Cypriot."

41.   Yennaris, *From the East*, 105-6.

42.   Elliott to Short, letter, 19 May 1977, FCO 9/2503, file WSC 014/3, pt. A.

43.   Martin Packard, *Getting It Wrong: Fragments from a Cyprus Diary 1964* (Milton Keynes: AuthorHouse, 2008), 1.   Packard is also very revealing about the FO role in encouraging and helping to draft the constitutional amendments.   He tells us: "It was agreed that the British government must deny any responsibility.   It suggested that it might be necessary to, if Nicosia

was found to have evidence of the part played by Clark [the high commissioner], to say that illness had led to his mental impairment" (338).

44.   British Embassy, Washington to Foreign Office, 7 July 1964, telegram 8541, FO 371/174766, file C-1205/2/G.

45.   Mallinson, *Cyprus, a Modern History*, 37.

46.   Ibid., 36. See also Hitchens, *Hostage to History*, 58-59.

47.   Packard, *Getting It Wrong*, 1.

48.   Ibid., 326.

49.   The author probably means *political realism/power politics*, since *realpolitik* most closely associated with the great European peacemaker, Bismarck, entailed the use of "soft power," rather than overtly threatening behavior and arm-twisting.

50.   Douglas Brinkley, "The Cyprus Question: Dean Acheson as Mediator," *Journal of the Hellenic Diaspora* 15, nos. 3 and 4 (fall-winter 1988).

51.   Mottershead to PUS, letter, 27 April 1964, enclosing brief for Defence and Overseas Policy (official) Committee D.O. (O) 64 26, with appendix, FO 371/29840.

52.   Van Coufoudakis, *Cyprus: A Contemporary Problem in Historical Perspective*, Minnesota Mediterranean and East European Monographs, no. 15 (Minneapolis: University of Minnesota, Modern Greek Studies, 2006), 83. See also Evriviades, where he writes: 'The US and Great Britain opposed the work of the UN designated mediator, the former president of Ecuador, Galo Plaza, and lobbied for the suppression of his report" ("The United States Strategic Interests," 234). The report can be found in *United Nations Security Council Official Records*, Supplement January-June 1965, S/6253 of 26 March 1965.

53.   *United Nations Security Council Document* 5/8348, 16 November 1967, in FCO 9/164, file CE 3/8.

54.   William Mallinson, "US Interests, British Acquiescence and the Invasion of Cyprus," *The British Journal of Politics and International Relations* 9, no. 3 (August 2007): 497-98.

55.   Hitchens, *Hostage to History*, 88.

56.   Mallinson, "US Interests," 498.

57.   Ibid.

58.   Mallinson, "The Year After," 82.

59.   Callaghan and Sauvagnargues, 19 July 1974, record of conversation, FCO 9/1984, file WSC 1/10, pt. E.

60.   Mallinson, "US Interests," 499.

61.   Mallinson, "1976," 15-16.

62.   Ibid.

63.   FCO *Diary of Events* of 14 and 15 August 1974, FCO 9/1909, file WSC 1/10, Pt. T.

64.   *Record of Telephone Conversation*, 5:00 p.m., Wednesday, 14 August 1975, PREM 1620.

65.   Costas Venizelos and Michalis Ignatiou, *Τα Μυστικά Αρχεία του Κίσιντζερ: Η απόφαση για τή διχοτόμηση* (Kissinger's secret files: The decision for partition) (Athens: A. A. Livani, 2002), 433-34.

66.   South East European Department, FCO, "British Interests in the Eastern Mediterranean," 11 April 1975, paper, FCO 46/1248, file DPI/516/1, in Mallinson, "The Year After."

67.   See FCO 9/2211, file WSC 18/1.

68.   Eugene T. Rossides, "British and US Responsibility for Turkey's Aggression in Cyprus," *Greek News*, 26 May 2008, *The Hellenic Voice*, 28 May 2008, and *The National Herald*, 31 May 2008.

69.   FCO brief for Kissinger's call on the Prime Minister of 10 December 1976, FCO 82/667, file AMU 020/548/7, pt. D.

70.   Dan Lindley and Caroline Wenzke, "Dismantling the Cyprus Conspiracy: The US Role in the Cyprus Crises of 1963, 1967, and 1974," University of Notre Dame, 16 May 2008. Draft awaiting comments. This sloppy and selective paper has apparently been written by two people, but the use of the first person is a bit of a giveaway. There is safety in numbers.

71.   Jan Asmussen, *Cyprus at War: Diplomacy and Conflict during the 1974 Crisis* (London and New York: I. B. Tauris, 2008), 9.

72.   CAB 129/178.

73.   Washington to FCO, 20 July 1974, FCO 9/1895, WSC1/1o, pt. F., telegram 3445.

74.   Tebbit to Wiggin, 30 December 1971, letter, FCO 82/62, file AMU 3/548/10.

75.   Laurence Stern, *The Wrong Horse: The Politics of Intervention and the Failure of American Diplomacy* (New York: Times Books/Quadrangle, 1977); and Thomas D. Boyatt, "Why Kissinger Was Wrong," in *The US and Cyprus: Double Standards and the Rule of Law*, ed. Eugene T. Rossides and Van Coufoudakis (Washington, D.C.: The American Hellenic Institute Foundation, 2002).

76.   See, for example, Farid Mirbagheri, *Cyprus and International Peacemaking* (London: Hurst and Company, 1998).

77.   Gordon to Secretary of State, 18 May 1977, "Archbishop Makarios Changes Horses," *Diplomatic Report* No. 232/77, FCO 9/2501.

78.   Prendergast to Fern, 30 September 1970, letter, FCO 9/1178, file WSC 10/14.

79.   Phillips to Foreign Secretary, Despatch, 24 August 1976, FCO 9/2376, file WSC 011/7.

80.   Private Secretary to Prendergast, 30 March 1978, letter, PREM 16/1671.

Chapter Three

1.   Judy Dempsey, *Financial Times*, 26 February 2003. See also Marios Evriviades' review of Claire Palley, *An International Relations Debâcle: The UN Secretary General's Mission of Good Offices in Cyprus 1999–2004* (Oxford and Portland, Ore.: Hart Publishing, 2005), *Mediterranean Quarterly* 17, no. 2 (spring 2006): 90, in which he attributes the following comment to Daniel Fried, a senior State Department official, made at an off-the-record briefing to Greek Americans: "When we were trying to persuade Turkey to

allow the passage of our troops through its territory into Northern Iraq, we offered Turkey two incentives, several billion dollars in grants and loans and Cyprus in the form of the Annan Plan." For some reason, Fried later denied having said what he was heard to have said. See also Gregory Copley, review of Palley, *An International Relations Debâcle*, *Defence and Foreign Affairs Strategic Policy*, issue 7 (July 2005), where he writes: "the rush to force a settlement on the Greek and Turkish Cypriots in 2004 was motivated and executed with deceit, stupidity and flagrant disregard for the sovereignty and freedom of peoples."

2.   See Palley, *An International Relations Debâcle*. The book gives a detailed and incisive account and analysis of the Annan Plan.

3.   See Perry Anderson, "The Divisions of Cyprus," *London Review of Books* 30, no. 8 (24 April 2008).

4.   See Gregory R. Copley, Turkish Strategic Imperatives and Western Intelligence Failures Led to the Collapse of Cyprus Resolution Talks," *Eastern Mediterranean Strategic Balance*, 24 June 2004, for an incisive analysis of the motives of the Turkish military.

5.   Ibid.

6.   Tassos Papadopoulos, "A People's Decision," *The National Interest Online*, The Nixon Center, Washington, D.C., 28 April 2004.

7.   Palley, *An International Relations Debâcle*, 34.

8.   *The Cyprus Question: A Brief Introduction*, 2^d ed. (Nicosia: Press and Information Office, Republic of Cyprus, 2006).

9.   David Hannay, *Cyprus: The Search for a Solution* (London and New York: I. B. Tauris, 2005), 246.

10.   Anderson, "The Divisions of Cyprus."

Chapter Four

1.   Attributed to Thomas Shadwell, in Ted Goodman, ed., *The Forbes Book of Business Quotations* (New York: Black Dog and Leventhal, 2007).

2.   James Pettifer, "We Have Been Here Before," *The World Today* 54, no. 4 (Chatham House, London, April 1998), 85. See also Michael McGwire, "Why did we bomb Belgrade?" *International Affairs* 76, no. 1 (Chatham House, London, January 2000), 6, in which McGuire writes that in 1998, the KLA was still classified as a terrorist organization.

3.   McGwire, "Why did we bomb Belgrade?," 14.

4.   Ibid., 13.

5.   Ibid., 22.

6.   Commander, British Forces Near East (Cyprus), report, 15 May 1975, WO 386/21.

7.   Hurst Hannum, "The Specter of Secession, Responding to Claims for Ethnic Self-Determination," *Foreign Affairs* 77, no. 2 (Washington, D.C., March/April 1998).

8.   I have borrowed this alliterative term from an eponymous article by Christopher Hitchens in *The Atlantic Online*, March 2003.

9.   V. N. Datta, "Examining the Great Divide," *The Sunday Tribune*, India, 1 April 2007.

10.   Arthur Herman, *Gandhi and Churchill* (London: Arrow Books, 2009), 569.

11.   Ministerial meeting of the North Atlantic Council, London, 10–11 May 1977, FCO brief, PREM 16/1624.

12.   Ibid. "It happens that the British Government's view of the issues is much closer to the Greek than the Turkish view. In particular, Britain supports the entitlement of islands to have a continental shelf."

13.   Mirbagheri, *Cyprus and International Peacemaking*, 48-49.

Chapter Five

1.   Marya Mannes, in Christopher Hitchens, "The Perils of Partition," *The Atlantic*, Boston, March 2003.

2.   Kumar, "The Troubled History of Partition." Kumar incisively and successfully attacks partition as a concept. See also Cable to Killick, minute attaching paper, 22 July 1974, in which the former wrote: "If the complete removal of the Turkish community from Cyprus has to be ruled out as impracticable (as the example of the Palestinians suggests may be the case), then at least a de facto and temporary partition of the island into clearly defined Greek and Turkish areas seems essential" (FCO 9/1916, file WSC1/11, pt. A).

3.   Chaim D. Kaufmann, "When All Else Fails," *International Security* 23, no. 2 (fall 1998), 151.

4.   See WO 386/21.

5.   Philip Gordon, "Cyprus: Divorce Could Precede Reconciliation," *International Herald Tribune*, 24 July 1997.

6.   Some might care to argue that in the case of Ireland, this no longer holds true. But who can be certain that calls for the unification of the island will not begin to mount again in some years?

7.   Hannum, "The Specter of Secession," 13-18.

8.   Kaufmann, "When All Else Fails," 156.

9.   Dan Lindley, "Historical, Tactical and Strategic Lessons from the Partition of Cyprus," *International Studies Perspectives*, no. 8 (2007): 224-41.

10.   See Thomas E. Hachey, *The Problem of Partition: Perils to World Peace* (Chicago: Rand McNally, 1972).

11.   Ibid.

12.   See Elena Baracani, "The EU's Impact on the Cyprus Conflict: Catalyst for Reunification or Partition of the Island?" *In Depth* 6, no. 2 (Nicosia, March-April 2009).

13.   Kypros Chrysostomides, *The Republic of Cyprus: A Study in International Law* (The Hague: Martinus Nijhoff, 2000), 342.

14.   Miltos Miltiadou and Van Coufoudakis, *The Cyprus Question: A Brief Introduction*, 3rd ed. (Nicosia: Press and Information Office, Republic of Cyprus, 2008), 12.

15.   McGwire, "Why did we bomb Belgrade?," 22.

16.   Weller, "The Rambouillet Conference on Kosovo," 251.

17.   Pritchard to Rogers, letter, 30 December 1965, CAB 164/1043.
18.   Pritchard to Rogers, letter, 25 January 1966, CAB 164/1043.
19.   *Position of United Kingdom Government in International Law in Relation to the Threatened Turkish Action against Cyprus*, 24 November 1967, FCO 27/166/MF/10/41.
20.   Ibid., "Background Note."
21.   Darwin to Parsons, minute, 28 February 1964, FO 371/174762, file C 1193/39.
22.   Steele (Legal Advisers, FCO) to Fearn, minute, 10 February 1971, FCO9/1374, file WSC 3/548/5.
23.   South East European Department, FCO, "British Interests in the Eastern Mediterranean," 11 April 1975, paper, FCO 46/1248, file DPI/516/1, in Mallinson, "The Year After."
24.   For a good set of arguments in favor of the rule of law, see Eugene T. Rossides, "Cyprus and the Rule of Law," *Syracuse Journal of International Law and Commerce* 17, no. 1 (spring 1991): 21-90.
25.   Olver to Goodison, letter, 4 March 1975, FCO 9/2159, WSC 1/7, pt. B.
26.   Batstone to Jones, minute, 21 March 1975, FCO 9/2159, WSC 1/7, pt. B.
27.   George Bush, "The Hard Work of Freedom," in Geraoid O'Tuthail, Simon Dalby, and Paul Routledge, eds., *The Geopolitics Reader* (London and New York: Routledge, 1998), 138.
28.   An interesting aside here is that shortly before Iraq's invasion of Kuwait, the U.S. ambassador to Baghdad, April Glaspie, told Saddam Hussein that it was not America's problem, thus encouraging him to invade. Yet more indicative of double standards was the West's support for Iraq's attack on, and war with, Iran. Similarly, the U.S. officials (State Department, etc.) were making statements that could only encourage Turkey to invade in 1974. There are plenty of those around.
29.   Weston to Goodison, minute, 8 May 1975, FCO9/2160, file WSC 1/7, pt. C.
30.   See David Vine, *Island of Shame: The Secret History of the US Military Base on Diego Garcia* (Princeton, N.J.: Princeton University Press, 2009), for a full account of this tawdry tale of backstage politics.
31.   Van Coufoudakis, *International Aggression and Violation of Human Rights*, Minnesota Mediterranean and East European Monographs, no. 17 (Minneapolis: University of Minnesota, Modern Greek Studies, 2008), 81. See also Ioannides, *In Turkey's Image*, for an authoritative account of the artificial transformation of occupied Cyprus.
32.   Some estimates have put the number of British in occupied Cyprus at 10,000. A precise figure is difficult to come by, given the illegality of the whole question.
33.   *Sunday Times*, 23 January 1977.
34.   See FCO 9/2251, file WSG 25/1.
35.   *Record of telephone conversation between Callaghan and Kissinger*, Wednesday, 14 August 1974, PREM 16/20.
36.   Pawley to Ford, letter, 29 July 1975, FCO 9/2162, file 1.7, pt. E.

37.   Miltiadou and Coufoudakis, *The Cyprus Question*, 3rd ed., 52.

38.   Michael Jansen, *War and Cultural Heritage: Cyprus after the 1974 Turkish Invasion*, Minnesota Mediterranean and East European Monographs, no. 14 (Minneapolis: University of Minnesota, Modern Greek Studies, 2005).

39.   D. McD. Gordon to Secretary of State, *Cyprus: Annual Review for 1975*, FCO 9/2377, file WSC 014/1.

40.   Vassilis Fouskas, *Cyprus: The Post-Imperial Constitution* (London: Pluto, 2009), 43.

41.   Ioannides, *In Turkey's Image*.

42.   Ibid., 44.

43.   I witnessed this at the UN Conference on Desertification, in Nairobi, August 1977.

Chapter Six

1.   Winston Churchill, speech to the House of Commons, 20 August 1940.

2.   Ahmet Djavit An, "The Turkish Cypriot Political Regime and the Role of Turkey," report sponsored and published by the Cyprus Council of the International European Movement (Nicosia, March 2004), 14.

3.   Edmonds to Secretary of State, "The Turkish Cypriot Administration," Diplomatic Report No. 503/72, 25 October 1972, FCO 9/1499, file WSC 1/12.

4.   Ibid.

5.   An, "The Turkish Cypriot Political Regime," 16.

6.   Anderson, "The Divisions of Cyprus."

7.   An, "The Turkish Cypriot Political Regime," 38.

8.   Ioannides, *In Turkey's Image*.

9.   Ibid., 55-56.

10.   An, "The Turkish Cypriot Political Regime," 17. The vice president of the (Turkish) Motherland Party, Bulent Akarcali, was quoted in *Yeni Demokrat*, 2 September 2001.

11.   Shener Levent, *Occupation* (Nicosia: N.p., 2004), 10-15.

12.   See, for example, the Council of Europe's Parliamentary Assembly's "Report on the Demographic Structure of the Cypriot Communities" (rapporteur Mr. A. Cuco), doc. No. 6589, 27 April 1992; and idem, "Report on the Colonisation by Turkish Settlers of the Occupied Part of Cyprus" (rapporteur Mr. J. Laakso), doc. No. 9799, 2 May 2003.

13.   Miltiadou and Coufoudakis, *The Cyprus Question*, 3rd ed., 51.

14.   Zachariades, "Transplanted Populations and the Problems Caused," 34.

15.   Ioannides, *In Turkey's Image*, 29.

16.   Christopher Hitchens, "Ankara Shows its Hand," *Slate* (New York), 20 April 2009.

17.   Palley, *An International Relations Debâcle*, 93. See also Miltos Miltiadou, *Toward a Unified Cyprus: The Myth of Turkish Cypriot Isolation*

(Nicosia: Press and Information Office, Republic of Cyprus, 2008), for an official, but nevertheless cogent, demolition of the isolation claim.

Chapter Seven

1.   Bill Mallinson, *Public Lies and Private Truths: An Anatomy of Public Relations* (London and New York: Cassell, 1996, and Athens: Leader Books, 2000), 103. The quote can be attributed to Benjamin Franklin.

2.   Old Greek saying.

3.   Meeting on Cyprus at the FCO, 19 September 1977, record, FCO 9/2505, file WSG 014/4.

4.   Miltiadou and Coufoudakis, *The Cyprus Question*, 3rd ed., 10.

5.   The president was quoted by Cyprus government spokesman Stefanos Stefanou at a book presentation at the University of Nicosia, 10 April 2009.

6.   Moore to Fuller, minute, 26 February 1964, FO 371/174762, file C 1015/1361.

7.   It could be argued that Cyprus had become a cat's paw long before then. I have chosen the time of the Crusades, however, because we see for the first time the overt involvement of northern powers.

8.   One might argue that the first major war fought on a global scale was the Seven Years' War, which therefore qualifies it as the first global war. What is considered the First World War was initially called the "Great War," not becoming widely known as the "First World War" until after what we now call the "Second World War." According to this scheme, the Napoleonic Wars constituted the second global war, and so on. The next putative global war will be the "Fifth World War." Whether anyone will be around to name it so is, of course, a moot point.

9.   The so-called European Rapid Reaction Force (ERRF), a child of the European Security and Defence Policy (ESDP), only operates "when NATO is not engaged." It is not therefore a true part of the Common Foreign and Security Policy (CFSP), one of the Maastricht pillars.

10.   Martin Walker, "Variable Geography," *International Affairs* 73, no. 3 (Chatham House, London, July, 2000): 472.

11.   Joseph S. Nye, "The American National Interest and Global Public Goods," *International Affairs* 78, no. 2 (Chatham House, London, April 2002): 243.

12.   Richard Norton-Taylor, *The Guardian*, 18 November 2002.

13.   These claims have even included Gavdos and Galopoulou, south of Crete.

14.   For a thoughtful look at Cyprus and the EU which includes a succinct view of Britain's interest, see Andreas Theophanous, *The Cyprus Question and the EU: The Challenge and the Promise* (Nicosia: Intercollege Press, 2004).

15.   *Cyprus Weekly*, 8 June 1990.

16.   Paul Vinocur, "French Accuse US of Meddling," *New York Times*, 13 December 2002.

17.   My own maxim.

18.   Vinocur, "French Accuse US of Meddling."

19.   Hitchens, "Ankara Shows its Hand."

20.   Gordon, "Cyprus: Divorce Could Precede Reconciliation."

21.   Philip H. Gordon and Henri J. Barkey, "Avoiding a Cyprus Crisis," Policy Brief no. 102 (Brookings Institution, Washington, D. C., July 2002).

22.   Henri J. Barkey and Philip H. Gordon, "A Good Deal for Cypriots— And for the World," *International Herald Tribune*, 9 September 2003.

23.   Ramsbotham to Secondé, letter, 3 March 1971, FCO 9/1371, file WSC 3/548/2.

Chapter Eight

1.   John Le Carré, *A Most Wanted Man* (London: Hodder and Stoughton, 2008), 280.

BIBLIOGRAPHY

Archivalia Consulted

Foreign Office (from 1970, Foreign and Commonwealth Office), British
National Archives Series FO 371 and 956, and FCO series 9
PREM (Prime Minister's Office)
DEFE (Ministry of Defence)
WO 386 (War Office)
CAB (Cabinet Office)

Works Cited

The following is a list only of those sources cited in the book. There
are many more publications that cannot be included. The fact that I have not
also cited from them (to avoid repetition) should not necessarily be seen as
implying that I do not consider them worthy of being read, but merely that I
have not attempted to stray too far from the theme of the book.

Albright, Madeleine. "The Testing of American Foreign Policy." *Foreign
        Affairs* 77, no. 6 (Washington, November/December 1998): 50-64.
An, Ahmet Djavit. "The Turkish Cypriot Political Regime and the Role of
        Turkey." Report sponsored and published by the Cyprus Council of
        the International European Movement. Nicosia, March 2004.
Anderson, Perry. "The Divisions of Cyprus." *London Review of Books* 30, no.
        8 (24 April 2008).
Asmussen, Jan. *Cyprus at War: Diplomacy and Conflict during the 1974
        Crisis.* London and New York: I. B. Tauris and Co. Ltd., 2008.
Baracani, Elena. "The EU Impact on the Cyprus Conflict: Catalyst for
        Reunification or Partition of the Island? *In Depth* 6, issue 2 (Nicosia,
        March-April 2009). Eelectronic newsletter of the Cyprus Center of
        European and International Affairs, affiliated with the University of
        Nicosia.
Boyatt, Thomas D. "Why Kissinger was Wrong." In *The US and Cyprus:
        Double Standards and the Rule of Law*, ed. Eugene T. Rossides and
        Van Coufoudakis, 323-25. Washington, D.C.: The American Hellenic
        Institute Foundation, 2002.

Brinkley, Douglas. "The Cyprus Question: Dean Acheson as Mediator." *Journal of the Hellenic Diaspora* 15, nos. 3 and 4 (fall-winter 1988): 5-18.

Buckle, B. E. *The Life of Benjamin Disraeli, Earl of Beaconsfield*. London: John Murray, 1920.

Bush, George. "The Hard Work of Freedom." In *The Geopolitics Reader*, ed. Geraoid O'Tuathail, Simon Dalby, and Paul Routledge, 136-38. London and New York: Routledge, 1998.

Carroll, Lewis. *Through the Looking-Glass*. 1872; London: Macmillan, 1996.

Copley, Gregory R. "Turkish Strategic Imperatives and Western Intelligence Failures Led to the Collapse of Cyprus Resolution Talks." GIS Special Topical Studies: Eastern Mediterranean Strategic Balance, http//128. 121.186.46./gis/online/SpecialStudies/EasternMed/Jun2404.htm, 24 June 2004.

———. "Identity Security as a Core Driver for the Reunification of Cyprus." Paper for Roundtable Discussion organised by the Research and Development Center, Intercollege, Nicosia, 18 October 2004.

———. "On Incompetence." Review of Claire Palley, *An International Relations Debacle*. *Defense and Foreign Affairs Strategic Policy*, no. 7 (July 2005): 15.

Coufoudakis, Van. *Cyprus: A Contemporary Problem in Historical Perspective*. Minnesota Mediterranean and East European Monographs, no. 15. Minneapolis: University of Minnesota, Modern Greek Studies, 2006.

———. *International Aggression and Violations of Human Rights: The Case of Turkey in Cyprus*. Minnesota Mediterranean and East European Monographs, no. 17. Minneapolis: University of Minnesota, Modern Greek Studies, 2008.

Coughlan, Reed. *Enosis and the British: British Official Documents 1878–1950*. Vol. 11 of *Sources for the History of Cyprus*, ed. Paul W. Wallace and Andreas G. Orphanides. Altamont, N.Y.: Greece and Cyprus Research Center, 2004.

Datta, V. N. "Examining the Great Divide." *The Sunday Tribune* (India), 1 April 2007.

Evriviades, Marios. "The United States Strategic Interests and the Policy of Partition." In *The United States and Cyprus: Double Standards and the Rule of Law*, 229-48. Washington, D.C.: American Hellenic Institute Foundation, Inc., 2002.

———. Review of Claire Palley, *An International Relations Debâcle*. *Mediterranean Quarterly* 17, no. 2 (spring 2006): 87-91.

Foot, Hugh. *A Start in Freedom*. London: Hodder and Stoughton, Ltd., 1964.

Fouskas, Vassilis. *Cyprus: The Post-Imperial Constitution*. London: Pluto, 2009.

Glenny, Misha. *The Balkans 1804–1999*. London: Granta Books, 1999.

Gordon, Philip. "Cyprus: Divorce Could Precede Reconciliation." *International Herald Tribune*, 24 July 1997.

———. "A Good Deal for Cypriots—and for the World." *International Herald Tribune*, 9 September 2003.

Gordon, Philip, and Henri Barkey. "Avoiding a Cyprus Crisis." Brookings Institution, Policy Brief no. 102. Washington, D.C., July 2002.

Hannay, David. *Cyprus: The Search for a Solution*. London and New York: I. B. Tauris, 2005.

Hachey, Thomas E. *The Problems of Partition: Perils to World Peace*. Chicago: Rand McNally, 1972.

Hannum, Hurst. "The Specter of Secession: Responding to Claims for Ethnic Self-Determination." *Foreign Affairs* 77, no. 2 (Washington, D.C., March/April 1998): 13-18.

Herman, Arthur. *Gandhi and Churchill*. London: Arrow Books, 2009.

Hill, Christopher. *The Changing Politics of Foreign Policy*. Basingstoke: Palgrave Macmillan, 2003.

Hitchens, Christopher. "What's Wrong with Partition? *New Statesman*, 21 August 1987, 21.

———. "The 'Green Line' Fallacy." *The Nation*, New York, 30 December 1996.

———. *Hostage to History*. London and New York: Verso, 1997.

———. "The Perils of Partition." *The Atlantic*, Boston, March 2003.

———. "Ankara Shows Its Hand." *Slate*, New York, 20 April 2009.

Holland, Robert. *Britain and the Revolt in Cyprus, 1954–1959*. Oxford University Press, 1998.

Ioannides, Christos. P. *In Turkey's Image: The Transformation of Occupied Cyprus into a Turkish Province*. New Rochelle, N.Y.: Aristides T. Caratzas, 1991.

James, Alan. "The UN Force in Cyprus." *International Affairs* 65, no. 3 (Royal Institute of Intenational Affairs, London, summer 1989).

Jansen, Michael. *War and Cultural Heritage: Cyprus after the 1974 Turkish Invasion*. Minnesota Mediterranean and East European Monographs, no. 14. Minneapolis: University of Minnesota, Modern Greek Studies, 2005.

Kaufmann, Chaim D. "When All Else Fails." *International Security* 23, no. 2 (fall 1998): 120-56.

Kissinger, Henry. *Nuclear Weapons and Foreign Policy*. New York: Harper and Brothers, 1957.

Kumar, Radha. "The Troubled History of Partition." *Foreign Affairs* 76, no. 1 (Washington, D.C., January/February 1997): 22-34.

Lee, Dwight E. *Great Britain and the Cyprus Convention of 1878*. Cambridge, Mass.: Harvard University Press, 1934.

Leigh, David, and Richard Norton-Taylor. "We Are Now a Client State." *The Guardian*, 17 July 2000.

Levent, Shener. *Occupation*. Nicosia, 2004.

Lindley, Dan. "Historical, Tactical and Strategic Lessons from the Partition of Cyprus." *International Studies Perspective*, no. 8 (May 2007): 224-41.

Lindley, Dan, and Caroline Wenzke. "Dismantling the Cyprus Conspiracy: The US Role in the Crises of 1963, 1967 and 1974." University of Notre Dame, 16 May 2008. Published on Lindley's website (www.allacademic.com/meta/p363717_index.html, 2009).

Litsas, Spyros. "The Origins of the Enosis Question in Cyprus." *Defensor Pacis*, issue 17 (Athens, July 2005).

Mallinson, William. *Portrait of an Ambassador: The Life, Times and Writings of Themistocles Chrysanthopoulos*. Athens, 1998.

———. "Turkish Invasions, Cyprus and the Treaty of Guarantee." *Synthesis-Review of Modern Greek Studies* 3, no. 1 (London School of Economics and Political Science, 1999): 39-48.

———. *Cyprus, a Modern History*. London and New York: I. B. Tauris, 2005; rev. ed. 2009.

———. "The Year After: Cyprus and the Shipwrecking of British Sovereignty." *Defensor Pacis*, issue 18 (Athens, July 2006): 65-89.

———. "US Interests, British Acquiescence and the Invasion of Cyprus." *The British Journal of Politics and International Relations* 9, no. 3 (August 2007): 494-508.

———. "1976: British Cyprus and the Consolidation of American Desires in the Eastern Mediterranean." *Defensor Pacis* 21 (Athens, September 2007): 14-29.

———. *Cyprus: Diplomatic History and the Clash of Theories in International Relations*. London and New York: I. B. Tauris, forthcoming.

McGwire, Michael. "Why did we bomb Belgrade?" *International Affairs* 76, no. 1 (Chatham House, London, January 2000): 1-23.

Miltiadou, Miltos. *Toward a Unified Cyprus: The Myth of Turkish Cypriot Isolation*. 3rd ed. Nicosia: Press and Information Office, Republic of Cyprus, 2008.

Miltiadou, Miltos, and Van Coufoudakis. *The Cyprus Question: A Brief Introduction*. 3rd ed. Nicosia: Press and Information Office, Republic of Cyprus, 2008.

Mirbagheri, Farid. *Cyprus and International Peacemaking*. London: Hurst and Company, 1998.

Nicolson, Harold. *Peacemaking 1919*. Universal Library Edition, no. 178. New York: Grosset and Dunlap, 1965.

Norton-Taylor, Richard. "The US Will Be Legislator, Judge and Executioner." *The Guardian*, 18 November 2002.

Nye, Joseph S. "The American National Interest and Global Public Goods." *International Affairs* 78, no. 2 (Chatham House, London, April 2002): 233-44.

O'Leary, Brendan. "Analysing Partition: Definition, Classification and Explanation." *MFPP Working Paper*, no. 27 (Institute for British-Irish Studies, Geary Institute for the Social Sciences, University College, Dublin, and Institute of Governance, Centre for International Borders Research, Queen's University, Belfast, 2006).

———. "Debating Partition: Justifications and Critiques." *MFPP Working Paper*, no. 28 (Institute for British-Irish Studies, University College,

Dublin and Institute of Governance, Centre for International Borders Research, Queen's University, Belfast, 2006).

O'Malley, Brendan, and Ian Craig. *The Cyprus Conspiracy*. London and New York: I. B. Tauris, 1999.

Packard, Martin. *Getting It Wrong: Fragments from a Cyprus Diary 1964*. Milton Keynes: AuthorHouse, 2008.

Papadopoulos, Tassos. Speech, seminar, Carnegie Endowment in Diplomacy, 4 August 1969. Published as *Cyprus, Developments and Realities*. Nicosia: Zavallis Press, 1969.

———. "A People's Decision." *The National Interest Online*, The Nixon Center, Washington, 28 April 2004.

Panteli, Stavros. *A History of Cyprus*. London: East-West Publications, 2000.

Palley, Claire. *An International Relations Debâcle: The UN Secretary General's Mission of Good Offices in Cyprus 1999–2004*. Oxford and Portland, Ore.: Hart Publishing, 2005.

Pettifer, James. "We Have Been Here Before." *The World Today* 54, no. 4 (Chatham House, London, April 1998).

Rice, Condoleezza. "Promoting the National Interest." *Foreign Affairs* 79, no. 1 (2000): 45-62.

Rossides, Eugene T. "Cyprus and the Rule of Law." *Syracuse Journal of International Law and Commerce* 17, no. 1 (spring 1991): 21-90.

———. "British and US Responsibility for Turkey's Aggression in Cyprus." *Greek News*, 26 May 2008, *The Hellenic Voice*, 28 May 2008, and *The National Herald*, 31 May 2008.

Rossides, Eugene T., and Van Coufoudakis, eds. *The US and Cyprus: Double Standards and the Rule of Law*. Washington, D.C.: The American Hellenic Institute Foundation, 2002.

Soulioti, Stella. *Fettered Independence: Cyprus, 1878–1964*. Minnesota Mediterranean and East European Monographs, no. 16. Minneapolis: University of Minnesota, Modern Greek Studies, 2006.

Stavrianos, L. S. *The Balkans since 1453*. 1958; London: C. Hurst and Co., 2000.

Stefanidis, Ioannis. *Isle of Discord*. London: Hurst and Company, 1999.

Stern, Laurence. *The Wrong Horse: The Politics of Intervention and the Failure of American Diplomacy*. New York: Times Books/Quadrangle, 1977.

Stevens, Robert. *Cyprus, A Place of Arms: Power Politics and Ethnic Conflict in the Eastern Mediterranean*. London: Pall Mall, 1966.

Taylor, A. J. P. *The Struggle for the Mastery of Europe, 1848–1918*. 1954; Oxford University Press, 1991.

Theophanous, Andreas. *The Cyprus Question and the EU: The Challenge and the Promise*. Nicosia: Intercollege Press, October 2004.

The Times Atlas of the World. Ref. ed. London: Times Books, 2003.

"Turkish Land Grab in Cyprus." Editorial. *New York Times*, 16 November 1983.

Venizelos, Costas, and Michalis Ignatiou. *Τα Μυστικά Αρχεία του Κίσιντζερ: Η απόφαση για τή διχοτόμηση* (Kissinger's secret files: The decision for partition). Athens: A. A. Livani, 2002.

Vine, David. *Island of Shame: The Secret History of the US Military Base on Diego Garcia*. Princeton, N.J.: Princeton University Press, 2009.

Vinocur, Paul. "French Accuse US of Meddling." *International Herald Tribune*, 13 December 2002.

Vryonis, Speros. *The Mechanism of Catastrophe: The Turkish Pogrom of 6–7 September 1955 and the Destruction of the Greek Community*. New York: Greekworks.com, 2005.

Walker, Martin. "Variable Geography: America's Mental Maps of a Greater Europe." *International Affairs* 73, no 3 (Chatham House, London, July 2000): 459-74.

Weller, Marc. "The Rambouillet Conference on Kosovo." *International Affairs* 75, no. 2 (Royal Institute of International Affairs, London, April 1999): 211-51.

West, Rebecca [Cecily Fairfield]. *Black Lamb and Grey Falcon*. Macmillan London Ltd., 1942; Edinbugh: Canongate Classics, 1993.

Wight, Martin. "Why Is There No International Theory?" In *Diplomatic Investigations*, ed. Herbert Butterfield and Martin Wight, 17-34. London: George Allen and Unwin Ltd., 1966.

Wright, Peter. *Spycatcher*. New York: Viking Penguin Inc., 1987.

Yennaris, Costas. *From the East*. London and Bath: Elliot and Thompson, 2003.

Yutang, Lin. *The Importance of Living*. 1938; London: Heinemann, 1976.

Zoellick, Robert B. "A Republican Foreign Policy." *Foreign Affairs* 79, no. 1 (2000): 63-78.

Zachariades, Michael A. "Transplanted Populations and the Problems Caused: Cyprus." Leiden University, September 2002, at www.aunitedcyprus. com.

Zaman. 16 March 2009, at www.todayszaman.com.

INDEX